T0271954

Routledge Revivals

The Iron Trade of Great Britain

Originally published in 1906, this volume presents a commercial review of the conditions and prospects of the iron and steel trades of Great Britain and its foreign competitors at the turn of the twentieth century. This title will be of interest to students of business and economics, as well as economic historians.

The Iron Trade of Great Britain

J. Stephen Jeans

Routledge
Taylor & Francis Group

First published in 1906
by Methuen & Co. Ltd

This edition first published in 2016 by Routledge
2 Park Square, Milton Park, Abingdon, Oxon, OX14 4RN
and by Routledge
711 Third Avenue, New York, NY 10017

Routledge is an imprint of the Taylor & Francis Group, an informa business

© 1906 Methuen & Co. Ltd

Publisher's Note
The publisher has gone to great lengths to ensure the quality of this
reprint but points out that some imperfections in the original copies may
be apparent.

Disclaimer
The publisher has made every effort to trace copyright holders and
welcomes correspondence from those they have been unable to contact.

A Library of Congress record exists under LC control number: 06029509

ISBN 13: 978-1-138-18790-0 (hbk)
ISBN 13: 978-1-315-64281-9 (ebk)

GROUP OF MIDDLESBROUGH BLAST FURNACES

THE IRON TRADE OF GREAT BRITAIN

BY

J. STEPHEN JEANS

SECRETARY TO THE BRITISH IRON TRADE ASSOCIATION
FORMERLY SECRETARY TO THE IRON AND STEEL INSTITUTE
MANAGING EDITOR OF "THE IRON AND COAL TRADES REVIEW"

WITH TWELVE ILLUSTRATIONS

METHUEN & CO.
36 ESSEX STREET W.C.
LONDON

First Published in 1906

CONTENTS

CONTENTS

LIST OF ILLUSTRATIONS

INTRODUCTION AND OUTLINE

THE purpose of the present volume is to present a commercial review of the conditions and prospects of the iron and steel trades of Great Britain, in relation to the rest of the world, and to the increasing demands for these materials at home and in all other countries. No attempt is made to enter upon a consideration of technical progress and conditions, which have been already dealt with in numerous important and valuable text-books, since the author in the year 1880 brought out the first general work on the steel industry.[1] Indeed, it may almost be said that to-day, with the standard works of Howe, Roberts-Austen, Campbell, and Harbord available, almost the last word has been said on the technical side of the iron and steel manufacture, while the recent important volume of reports on *American Industrial Conditions and Competition*, drawn up by the Commission of the British Iron Trade Association, in 1902–3, brings pretty well up to date the distinguishing characteristics of American practice, and shows the differences of conditions between the United States and our own country.

It is otherwise with the more strictly commercial aspects of the iron trade situation. The great tariff controversy that has recently raged, and is still raging; the importance

[1] *Steel: Its History, Manufacture, Properties, and Uses.*

vii

that has been attached in and through that controversy to the subject of dumping; the increasing tendency of foreign countries to shut out British manufactures from their markets by higher tariffs; the general diffusion of, and the movement which aims at regulating production and prices by, cartels and syndicates; the increasing importance attached to the possession of adequate supplies of suitable raw materials; the continuing keenness and success of foreign competition in outside markets; the extraordinary advances that foreign nations have lately made in filling home contracts; the frequency with which municipalities and county councils have accepted the tenders of foreign producers rather than those of home origin; and the general uneasiness that prevails as to the future, alike from the point of view of raw materials and from that of the increasing effectiveness of foreign competition—all these conditions and influences combine to invest with exceptional, if not unprecedented, interest the questions that cluster around and depend upon the general commercial situation dealt with in these pages.

It is probably the simple truth to say that there is no industry carried on in the world that is more liable to, and affected by, foreign competition than that of iron and steel. These products are universal needs. They are produced on a very large scale. The business is liable to extraordinary fluctuations. There is a wide range within which profits may be made greater or less, in harmony with efficiency of administration and general organising capacity. Probably no industry has made so many men wealthy. The term "ironmaster" has almost become a synonym in general parlance for a rich man. The example of Carnegie is regarded as more or less typical.

In all this there is a great liability to misapprehension. The iron trade has undoubtedly produced a good many millionaires; but then, no other industry is followed on so vast a scale, or involves such a great expenditure of capital. Great profits are no doubt frequently secured, but these often coincide with equally large losses. Mr. Carnegie has truly said that the iron trade is either prince or pauper. Men who become rich are talked about. Men who go into the bankruptcy court are liable to be forgotten. Looking back on the history of the iron trade, I am disposed to say that the one is almost as common an experience as the other.

The belief that the iron trade is a source of perennial riches is no doubt largely responsible for the recent increase of foreign competition. Up to the year 1875, Belgium was our only real competitor. The United States could not produce cheaply enough to offer any chance of success in this field, and Germany did not seriously try conclusions in neutral markets until some years later, nor did she enter our home markets to any extent worth speaking of until quite a recent date. For the last four years British iron and steel imports have averaged over a million tons a year, of which nearly two-thirds have been furnished by Germany, and the remainder by Belgium, Sweden, and the United States. In foreign markets the competition of these countries is perhaps even more severe than in our home markets. The same remark applies to our colonial markets. Twenty years ago we had a virtual monopoly of our colonial markets. To-day we still dominate in Australia and India, but in Canada we only provide about thirty per cent. of the total, the remainder being provided by the United States and Germany.

Nevertheless, British iron and steel are still supplied to most foreign countries, and to all our colonies, on a greater or smaller scale. Our total iron and steel exports have not in any one intermediate year exceeded the exports of twenty years ago, but we can hardly be said to have entirely lost any one market, despite the influence of hostile tariffs and bounties, and the strenuousness of the efforts made by our competitors in all directions. This is satisfactory so far as it goes, but it is necessary to add that our hold on foreign markets is loosening year by year, while we retain a firmer grip on our colonial markets, and find our trade with them, in the main, an increasing one. The general opinion appears to be that our main reliance must in the future be on our colonial business, and in that view I fully concur, up to a certain point. But it will not be overlooked that the time is certain to ultimately arrive when our principal colonial possessions, and India, will largely supply their own needs. At present the total annual iron and steel consumption of our colonial possessions and India may be taken at about two and a half millions of tons, and it is increasing very rapidly. This is fully recognised in at any rate four different groups, and hence in India, Canada, Australasia, and South Africa, many projects have been mooted or organised for establishing a home industry. Indeed, so far as Canada is concerned, there are already in existence plants equal to producing practically all the pig iron that the Dominion can consume, but the conditions under which they are worked have not hitherto enabled those plants to displace the imported article. In India there is only one considerable establishment engaged in producing pig iron, but others have been projected, as well as steel plants of importance, and are likely soon to be translated into fact. In Australasia and South Africa there are not as yet either iron or steel works worth speaking of, but both groups of colonies are anxious to see them established, and have offered inducements to that end.

The principal British iron-producing districts are Cleveland, in North Yorkshire, yielding nearly five and a half million tons annually; Lincolnshire, Northamptonshire, and Leicestershire, together yielding four and a quarter million tons; and Cumberland and North Lancashire, with an output of over one and a half million tons.

The Cleveland ore occurs in the form of a bed about ten feet thick in the Middle Lias, and is worked by true underground mining; it contains on an average about 30 per cent. of metal.

The bed of brown iron ore in Lincolnshire, Northamptonshire, and Leicestershire, forms part of the Inferior Oolite, and the workings are mainly open. The percentage of iron on an average is about 31. In Cumberland and Lancashire the ore is a red hematite which occurs in the form of huge irregular masses in the Carboniferous Limestone; this is the richest ore of the country, yielding more than 50 per cent. of metal.

So far as British plants are concerned, the total number of pig-iron works in operation in Great Britain is 123, and these works have about 570 blast furnaces, of which the number in operation at any one time varies from 340 to 350. The total output of pig iron during recent years has varied from about eight million tons to about nine and a half million tons a year; the consumption of iron ore ranges from about nineteen to twenty-two million tons; and the coal consumed varies from sixteen to eighteen million tons. The quantity of iron ore actually raised in the United Kingdom ranges from twelve and a half to fifteen million tons, and the imports range from six to seven and a half million tons.

During the last thirty years the blast-furnace plants in Great Britain have been very much improved. This has involved a demolition of many of the old furnaces which were not suited to the conditions of the present time. In 1873 the total number of blast furnaces in blast in Great Britain was 683, whereas in 1904 the number was only 340, and yet the furnaces of 1904 made considerably more iron than the much larger number blowing in 1873. Indeed, the furnaces of the present time may be taken as equal to producing twice the average of those of only a quarter of a century ago. The largest output of British pig iron in any one year was 9,421,435 tons. This figure was attained in 1899 with 411 furnaces in blast.

The following table gives the output of pig iron, Bessemer and open-hearth steel, and puddled iron, in each leading district of Great Britain in 1904 :—

IRON AND STEEL OUTPUT OF LEADING BRITISH DISTRICTS
IN 1904, IN TONS

DISTRICT	PIG IRON	STEEL	PUDDLED IRON
Cleveland . . .	2,234,345 ...	1,229,322 ...	106,880
Scotland . . .	1,339,000 ...	1,020,000 ...	207,350
Wales . . .	779,600 ...	1,068,761 ...	7,000
Durham . . .	981,100	Included in Cleveland	Included in Cleveland
W. Cumberland . .	551,300 ...	370,500 ...	—
Lancashire . . .	522,900 ...	342,100 ...	130,715
Lincolnshire . .	321,400	Included in S. & W. Yorkshire	Nil
Derbyshire . .	292,400 ...	Nil ...	31,662
Northamptonshire .	223,900 ...	Nil ...	Nil
Notts and Leicester .	310,800 ...	Nil ...	Nil
Staffordshire . .	573,100 ...	420,000 ...	338,398
S. and W. Yorkshire .	263,413 ...	533,362 ...	107,997
Other districts . .	385,400 ...	— ...	123,226
Totals of U.K.	8,562,658	5,026,879	936,228

It will be observed that the production of steel in Great Britain in 1904 was as much as 5,026,879 tons, or nearly six times the output of puddled iron. This is an entire reversal of the conditions that existed thirty years ago, for the total make of British puddled iron in 1875 was close on three million tons, while the output of steel was under a million tons.

The production of British steel in the first half of 1905 was at the rate of close on six million tons a year, and marked one of the greatest strides that the industry has hitherto made in a single year. This result is largely due to the notable improvement that has taken place in open-hearth steel-making practice. Until about fifteen years ago, the general practice was to use five-ton or ten-ton furnaces, and the average annual output of ingots per furnace varied from 5,000 to 7,000 tons. To-day the average size of the furnaces in use will probably be thirty tons, and the average annual output per furnace is not likely to be under 12,000 tons, and is in some cases considerably more. In the future this output is certain to be much exceeded by the larger use of furnaces of the Talbot or Bertrand-Thiel type, as now adopted at Frodingham, Dowlais, Dudley, Brymbo, and Cargo Fleet Works.

As the output of steel has increased, so has the output of puddled iron declined in most ironmaking countries. Cleveland and South Staffordshire have been the greatest sufferers in the British Isles from this movement. In these two districts taken together, the output of puddled iron at its maximum was close on two million tons, whereas to-day it does not exceed half a million tons. Much the same conditions have in the same interval prevailed in competitive countries. The explanation is easy. Iron is a fibrous material which has its strength mainly in one direction, and has no great range of physical conditions, whereas steel is a crystalline substance, having its strength equally in every direction, and having physical conditions which range from the hardness of the diamond to the toughness of leather. Hence steel is not only applicable to a much greater variety of uses, but is usually endowed with a much longer life.

It has been proved by many years' experience that steel

has three times the life of wrought iron for railway purposes, and this fact led at an early stage in the history of the Bessemer process to the application of its products to the manufacture of steel rails. On the other hand, the greater softness that can be secured in steel plates and sheets adapts them much better than those of wrought iron for shipbuilding, tin-plates, and other important uses.

IMPORTS AND EXPORTS

The following table gives the totals of the imports and exports of iron and steel as recorded for the leading producing countries in 1904, in tons :—

COUNTRY	TOTAL IMPORTS	TOTAL EXPORTS
United Kingdom . .	1,291,880 ...	3,266,248
United States . .	266,397 ...	1,167,674
Germany . . .	420,282 ...	3,036,473
France	190,480 ...	588,115
Belgium . . .	622,200 ...	794,911

A mere glance at these figures will show that the United Kingdom enjoys the distinction of being the largest importer and exporter alike among the iron - producing countries of the world. This position it has held for more than a century; but of late years other nations, and more especially Germany, have been approaching British export figures, and it seems not improbable that the time may speedily come when Great Britain will have to yield up its supremacy as an iron-exporting nation, as it has already resigned its pride of place as the greatest iron-producer in the world.

The imports and the exports of the leading countries vary, however, so greatly from year to year that it is impossible to arrive at an accurate estimate of the conditions and the possibilities of foreign trade from the records of any one year. This consideration of late years has more especially applied to the United States and Germany.

Within three recent years the imports of iron and steel into the United States have in one year been about five times as much as in another, while the exports from that country have in one year been more than three times the volume reached in another. Similarly, in the case of Germany, the iron and steel exports of 1902 were 120 per cent. greater than those of only two years before. British trade is not liable to quite such large fluctuations, the greatest variation between minimum and maximum exports on the last six years having been no more than 24 per cent. in respect of manufactured iron and steel, and 75 per cent. in respect of pig iron.

The following short table summarises the exports of the four principal iron-producing countries in respect of the leading descriptions produced and sent abroad, showing Britain's notable supremacy in respect of exports of pig iron, plates and sheets, tin-plates and rails, and the leading position held by Germany in respect of general merchant products and wire :—

EXPORTS OF LEADING DESCRIPTIONS OF IRON AND STEEL

	Great Britain	Germany	United States	Belgium
	TONS	TONS	TONS	TONS
Pig iron . . .	813,000 ...	418,072 ...	49,025 ...	24,666
General merchant iron .	211,000 ...	419,555 ...	55,400 ...	380,005
Plates and sheets . .	538,000 ...	293,000 ...	55,205 ...	91,369
Tin and black plates .	421,000 ...	177 ...	7,898 ...	2,186
Blooms and billets, etc.	177,000 ...	396,000 ...	314,324 ...	4,990
Rails	525,000 ...	378,611 ...	416,200 ...	175,114
Wire, wire nails and rods	61,000 ...	254,000 ...	151,250 ...	18,226

France, in 1904, exported 190,792 tons of pig iron, 64,143 tons of finished iron, and 205,239 tons of steel, not including re-exports from duty-free imports of crude material, which reached 127,931 tons. No other nation has so far entered the ranks of iron-exporting countries to any extent worth speaking of, if Sweden be excepted ;

but Swedish products are more or less *sui generis*. It is necessary to add that foreign competition, and more especially on the part of the United States and Germany, is increasing very greatly, and that it has more than doubled in volume within the last fifteen years.

Owing to this paramount fact, attention has been given in the pages that follow to the international rather than the more strictly local and national aspects of the iron trade of Great Britain, as being the more important field of inquiry, both to those engaged in the trade and to the community as a whole. Hence the last few chapters of the present work, in which the more general aspects of the iron trade situation are considered.

THE
IRON TRADE OF GREAT BRITAIN

CHAPTER I

A SHORT HISTORICAL RETROSPECT

THE history of the iron trade of Great Britain is full
of technical, industrial, and antiquarian interest.
Most of the iron-producing centres of to-day have distinguishing records of their own, which come up to quite
recent times. But certain localities were distinguished in
respect of the iron industry almost from a prehistoric
period. The vestiges found in many localities prove that
the iron industry was carried on in Scotland, in Cumberland and North-west Lancashire, in Wales, and in other
localities, some hundreds of years ago. The practical and
historical period of development may be said to begin
with the early part of the eighteenth century. At that
time manufactured iron was virtually the only commodity
produced or used. Steel was, indeed, manufactured in
several places, and its history is of great interest both to
the metallurgist and to the antiquary; but to the business
man and the ordinary reader it is a matter of but little
concern.

In the eighteenth century the iron industry was chiefly
carried on in South Staffordshire, Scotland, Shropshire,
Durham, South Wales, and South and West Yorkshire.

B

In many cases the works were far from the sea and from one or other—sometimes from both—of the chief raw materials employed.   The conditions under which the iron industry of that early period was carried on are more or less fully set forth in nearly all of the many treatises that deal with its technology and commerce. It is not therefore necessary to go far into the matter here.   There were numerous small forges scattered up and down the country, which chiefly produced bar iron for smiths' use, hoops, sheets, rods, angles, and a few other products.   Rails were not produced to any extent until about 1830, when the railway system had entered on its great career.   Ship plates came into vogue at a considerably later date.   These two products have now for many years been produced in this country on a larger scale than any other.   Sheets—plain, galvanised, and corrugated—are of still later origin and growth ; and so also with tin plates, although Yarranton makes it clear that they were to some extent manufactured more than a hundred years ago.

The iron trade appears to have been marked by the following notable movements or changes, which have been the leading landmarks in its history :—

1. The improvements introduced into the puddling process by Cort and Rogers.

2. The successful adoption of raw coal in the blast furnace by Dud Dudley and others.

3. The discovery and application of the hot blast by Neilson, of Glasgow.

4. The discovery and application of the Cleveland ironstone about 1845, and the establishment of the iron trade of Tees-side about 1850.

5. The discovery and application of the Bessemer process of steel manufacture in 1856.

6. The discovery and application of the open-hearth

process of steel manufacture by the Siemens Brothers between 1864 and 1867.

7. The development of the capacity of production in the blast furnaces of Cleveland and other districts between 1867 and 1875.

8. The announcement and subsequent improvement of the basic process of steel manufacture by Mr. Sidney G. Thomas, assisted by Mr. E. Windsor Richards and Mr. Edward P. Martin, between 1879 and 1883.

9. The general improvement and more economical working of blast and rolling-mill engines and rolling mills, whereby much greater yields were obtained at a lower cost.

10. The introduction in the United States of many new methods, processes, and appliances, whereby vastly larger yields of both iron and steel were obtained, and great economy of labour cost was effected.

These are all more or less strictly technical changes, innovations, and improvements. They coincided with, and were more or less the primary causes of almost, if not quite, equally remarkable commercial developments, of which the more notable were :—

1. The cheapening of the cost of producing both pig iron and steel—a movement which was most pronounced in Great Britain in the period 1860–70.

2. The building up of a large export trade in iron and steel products, whereby the volume shipped from British ports increased from 91,000 tons in 1820 to 4,353,000 tons in 1882.

3. The growth of a heavy import trade in the same products, which, amounting to only 57,000 tons of all kinds in 1860 and to 276,000 tons in 1880, had increased to about 1,300,000 tons in 1903.

4. The development of a great business in the importation of foreign ores, which increased from 114,000 tons in

1868 to about 3,000,000 tons in 1888, and to over 7,000,000 tons in 1899.

5. A rapid decline in the output of manufactured iron, which fell from 2,841,000 tons in 1882 to a little over a million tons in 1892, and to less than a million tons in 1902.

6. A striking concurrent advance in the output of open-hearth steel, which was less than half a million tons in 1883, and rose to over three million tons in 1903.

7. A notable advance in the output of a given plant in every branch of the iron and steel industries, whereby the production of pig iron, Bessemer steel, open-hearth steel, and finished products, was fully doubled, and in many cases was much more than doubled.

8. The rapid expansion of the American and Continental iron industries, leading within the last ten years to a great increase of competition and to the more or less considerable invasion of British markets.

9. The development during recent years of the system known as dumping, whereby Germany, Belgium, and the United States have within six years nearly trebled their united exports of iron and steel to Great Britain.

10. The building up of a large export trade to the United States, which in several years took from us more than a million tons of iron and steel annually, and the subsequent almost entire loss of that important market by increasingly hostile tariffs and by increasingly successful manufacturing enterprise by American producers.

11. The extraordinarily large and rapid increase in the world's demand for iron and steel, whereby the total output of pig iron in all countries rose from 20,000,000 tons in 1883 to 44,000,000 tons in 1903, and the concurrent advance in the world's demands for steel, which rose from less than 7,000,000 tons in 1883 to more than 36,000,000 tons in 1903.

While these seem to the writer to have been the more notable phenomena distinguishing the technical and commercial growth of the iron and steel industries, it is not to be taken for granted that they stand alone. Indeed, the changes that have taken place have been so numerous and so far-reaching that it is difficult to assign limits to their influence or to weigh their individual dimensions.

The course of the iron trade has had an important influence on, and has in its turn been notably affected by, the various great economic movements and changes that have happened during the last century. The most important event in the development of a demand for iron was naturally the introduction and growth of the railway system. In the United Kingdom nearly a million and a half tons are annually consumed for railway purposes. In the United States the corresponding consumption is probably well on to five million tons, including rolling stock of all kinds as well as permanent way. About 1835 an impetus was given to the British iron trade by the beginning of the railway era in the United States, which had then to purchase most of its materials in this country. The ups and downs of the trade were in those days almost as varied as in later years, despite the relatively limited extent of the trade. In 1843, for example, the price of manufactured iron was extremely low, and conditions generally were much depressed, but in the following year the railway " mania " caused a large and a rapid recovery, which continued over the following year. In 1851 the holding of the First International Exhibition in London called attention to the technical development of the trade, and two years later there was a large increase in British iron exports, especially to the United States, which took from us 43 per cent. more exports than in 1851. In 1856 much attention was excited in the trade, and called to it from outside, by the announcement of the discovery of the Bessemer process; and the almost concurrent commencement of railway construction in India and in some of our own colonies contributed to the interest and to the prospects of a largely increased demand. In 1857, for the first time, considerable contracts were placed in this country for Russian railways, then just being built on an important scale. Trade continued to increase more slowly in the next few years, nor was it until the close of the American Civil War that it received a further notable fillip. That event happened in 1865, and it coincided with a very serious and prolonged strike of iron-workers in both the North of England and the Midlands, the happy issue of which was the Board of Conciliation and Arbitration through which ironworkers' wages have since been regulated. About 1869 extensive railway building operations were adopted on the Continent, but these were checked in July, 1870, by the declaration of war between France and Germany. When peace was concluded in the following year, both nations desired to proceed with their railway and other improvement schemes; and as they had not the necessary resources for providing the required materials, very large contracts were placed in Great Britain, which was the only country that at that time was in a position to execute them. The almost simultaneous expansion of general trade and railways in other countries caused the nearest approach to a coal and iron famine that we have ever known. In 1871 there was a rapid rise in prices, and in 1872 and 1873 the general range of values for all commodities was higher than it has ever been since. The prices of iron ore, coal, coke, pig iron, and manufactured iron and steel of all kinds, rose from 100 per cent. to 200 per cent. The cost of labour rose very largely at the same time, until the wages of coal miners and ironworkers were more or less doubled in amount. This movement led to much trouble in the years that immediately followed. About 1874 trade became depressed, and the depression lasted until 1879. Many strikes took place in the interval, following chiefly on demands for reduced wages. The situation was rendered more difficult by the development, almost for the first time in our modern industrial history, of foreign competition, which, beginning with Belgium, extended in course of time to Germany, France, and other countries. Between 1877 and 1879 this competition was much felt. In 1879, however, trade took a turn for the better, and the improvement continued until the end of 1880, during which time prices rose to a higher level than had been known since 1873. The next few years were marked by notable depression, especially the years 1885–7. In that time many failures took place, prices fell to an almost unknown level, exports fell off considerably, money was tight, wages were low, and all the usual accompaniments of severe depression were rampant. This was, perhaps, on the whole, the most dismal period that the iron and steel trades have ever known. It coincided not only with a great increase in foreign competition, but with striking and revolutionary changes in processes and products. The more important of these were the substitution of steel for iron in respect of shipbuilding, and many other applications, and the increasing adoption and success of the open-hearth process of steel manufacture, initiated and carried to a practical issue by Messrs. William and Frederick Siemens.

Again in 1889, almost exactly ten years after the previous reaction had begun, business took a turn for the better, and during that year and the year 1890 there was not much to complain of. Foreign trade improved, home demands increased, and prices all round advanced. The improvement, however, was short-lived. In 1891 it had clearly spent itself. In 1892 trade was again seriously depressed. In the following three years it was unsatis-

factory, but in 1896 it took a change for the better; and
the next five years witnessed perhaps the longest and, on
the whole, the most satisfactory revival that the iron trade
has ever known. During this period the make of British
pig iron increased from 7·7 million to 9·4 million tons.
This advance coincided with a corresponding increase
from 9·4 to 13·6 million tons in the case of the United
States, and from 5·4 to 8·1 million tons in the case
of Germany, while nearly all other iron-making countries
had similar records. The make of pig iron throughout
the world in these five years increased from a little over
thirty to about forty million tons.

In the year 1806 there were 133 ironworks of all kinds
in Great Britain. In Scotland 23,240 tons of iron were
produced from twenty-seven blast furnaces, of which
eighteen were in operation, being an average of 1,291 tons
per year. In 1830 the quantity of pig iron produced in
Scotland had increased to 40,000 tons. The invention
of the hot blast by Neilson was patented in 1829, and
gave the trade a great stimulus from that date.

In the year 1800 the British make of pig iron was less
than 150,000 tons, and the average make of pig iron per
furnace was about 2,000 tons. In 1899 the British make
of pig iron was over 9,300,000 tons, and the average make
of pig iron in the country generally—disregarding a few
small furnaces whose make is exceptionally small—may be
taken at 30,000 tons per furnace. But in the United
States this annual average output has been considerably
more than doubled, and it is being increased every year in
our own country.

Previous to Neilson's invention being applied at the
Clyde works, when iron was made by means of the cold
blast, a single ton required as fuel to reduce it 8 tons 1¼ cwt.
of coal converted into coke. In the first six months of the
following year, when the air was heated by Neilson's

system to 300 degrees Fah., one ton of pig iron required 5 tons 3½ cwt. of coal converted into coke, representing an economy of 2 tons 18 cwt. on the manufacture of a single ton. From this figure must be deducted the 8 cwt., or thereabout, of coal used in heating the blast. But at this time the hot blast was only in its infancy, and its full advantages had not been ascertained. Scrivenor tells us that about the beginning of 1831 Mr. Dixon, proprietor of the Clyde Ironworks, substituted raw coal for coke, and from that time—the change having resulted in complete success—the use of coke has been almost entirely abandoned by the Scotch ironmasters. During the first six months of the year 1833 one ton of iron was made with 2 tons 5¼ cwt. of raw coal, which, with 8 cwt. of coal required to heat the blast, gives 2 tons 13¼ cwt. of coal required to make a ton of iron, as compared with 8 tons 1¼ cwt. of coal required previous to 1829 under the operation of the cold blast. Sixty-five years ago Scotch coal was procurable at the pit's mouth for 3s. per ton, and although the price was low, the economy of nearly six tons of coal per ton of iron made, resulting from the hot blast, was sufficient to cause a revolution in the trade.

The first public attempt to examine scientifically the value of increased weight and capacity in blast furnaces appears to have been made by Mr. Charles Cochrane, who, in a paper read before the Society of Mechanical Engineers, pointed out that the actual quantity of coke necessary in a blast furnace was that demanded for the reduction and carburising of the iron, and this he estimated at 17·43 cwt. per ton of metal. Mr. Cochrane, in the discussion which followed the reading of his paper, expressed a hope that by still further increasing the dimensions of the furnace, enough heat might be conveyed into it to enable a ton of Cleveland iron to be produced with 13 cwt. of coke—a pious hope not hitherto realised.

CHAPTER II

THE RAW MATERIALS OF THE BRITISH IRON INDUSTRY

IRON ORE SUPPLIES

THE basis of all supremacy in the iron trade is adequate supplies of cheap raw material. That material consists of iron ores on the one hand and of coal and coke on the other. The iron ore problem is, however, by far the more important; first, because there is a much less ample supply of good iron ores than of good coal; and next, because while $1\frac{1}{2}$ ton of coal will usually suffice for the production of a ton of pig iron, the average consumption of ore is over two tons, and in a good many cases, including our own Cleveland district, Luxembourg, Alsace, and Alabama (U.S.), approaches, and even exceeds, three tons.

The greatest known reserves of ore of a high class, cheaply mined and readily smelted, are those of the Lake Superior region, in the United States. In this region there are five different iron ore ranges, known severally as the Marquette, the Vermilion, the Gogebic, the Mesabi, and the Menominee. These five regions furnished the blast furnaces of the United States in 1903 with nearly twenty-seven million tons of ore, or four times as much as the quantity provided by them only twenty-five years before. The only other district in the United States that produces iron ore on a large scale is that of Alabama, which, however, has never in any one year produced much over 3½ million tons. Iron ores are produced in twenty-two other states and territories, but on a small scale, none of them equalling a million tons a year.

The iron ore supplies of Great Britain are derived partly from home deposits and partly by imports from foreign countries and British colonies. The home output varies from twelve to fourteen million tons a year, of which nearly one half is furnished by the Cleveland district in North Yorkshire. The mines or deposits are classified under the three categories of the Coal Mines Act, under which the supplies provided exceed one half of the whole; the Metalliferous Mines Act, under which West Cumberland, etc., provide about 1¾ million tons a year; and the Quarries Act, under which Lincolnshire, Northamptonshire, and one or two other districts, provide us with about 4½ million tons annually. The proportion of mineral contributed under the Quarries Act has recently been increasing materially.

The iron ore imports of Great Britain are mainly obtained from the north of Spain, but increasing quantities are being mined in and exported from the southern ports. The total quantity imported has been quadrupled within the last twenty years, and now amounts to about 6½ million tons annually, of which Spain provides about four-fifths. The other countries of supply are mainly Greece, Italy, Algeria, and Sweden, although smaller contributions are made by about a dozen other foreign countries, and nine or ten British possessions. In some quarters an impression seems to prevail that in course of time our own colonies will send us increasing quantities of iron ore. This is possible. Newfoundland has already sent up to about 90,000 tons in a year. But most of the other colonies are too remote to justify the expectation that much will come of this business unless freights can be reduced.

The bulk of the Swedish ores has hitherto been shipped to Germany, and this is likely to continue; but during the past ten years there has been a steadily increasing importation of Lapland iron ores into Great Britain, more particularly the low phosphoric " A " grade (for hematite and for open-hearth acid steel), and the intermediate " C " grade (for mixing with native ores and for open-hearth basic steel). As long as the Swedish mines were restricted to the shipment of their ores from the Port of Lulea, in the Gulf of Bothnia, the British shipments were confined principally to the north-east coast of England and the east coast of Scotland, but since then the commencement of the new Port of Narvik, on the west coast of Norway (Ofoten Fjord), has liberated the ores from the extensive deposits of Kiirunavaara, which are a valuable source of supply for the British iron trade, consisting as they do principally of phosphoric ore, of various grades, containing from about $1\frac{1}{4}$ per cent. to 4 per cent. of phosphorus.

From the fact that the ores imported into Great Britain are received through more than twenty different ports, it will be understood that such ores are pretty widely used. Wales is almost exclusively dependent upon them. Scotland now imports more ore than she raises at home. West Cumberland and North-west Lancashire depend on imports for nearly one half their total supply, although until within the last fifteen years imported ores were almost unknown in this region. Finally, the Cleveland district, which has vast ore deposits of its own, now imports annually nearly two million tons of foreign ores, which of late years have been used in increasing quantities. The total quantity of British pig annually made from imported ores varies from 3 to $3\frac{1}{2}$ million tons. Such ores are almost wholly non-phosphoric, and are used to produce what in the United States is known as Bessemer, and in this country as hematite or acid pig iron.

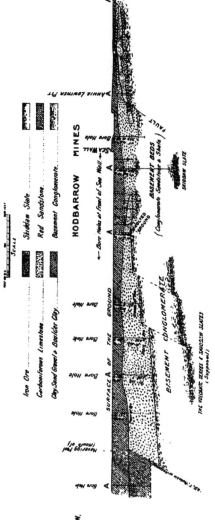

SECTION OF HODBARROW MINES

W.

E.

HODBARROW MINES

SCALE

Iron Ore
Carboniferous Limestone
Clay, Sand, Gravel & Boulder Clay

Silurian Slate
Red Sandstone
Basement Conglomerate

ANNIE LOWTHER PIT

SEA WALL

Bore Hole

Bore Marks at Front of Sea Wall

FAULT

BASEMENT BEDS
(Conglomerate Sandstone & Shale)

SKIDDAW SLATE

SURFACE OF THE GROUND

Bore Hole

Bore Hole

Bore Hole

Bore Hole

BASEMENT CONGLOMERATE

THE VOLCANIC SERIES & SKIDDAW SLATES
(Supposed)

Haverigg Pool
(mouth of)

Bore Hole

For many years Great Britain was the largest producer of iron ores as well as of pig iron and finished products among the leading iron-producing nations. From this pride of place she was dislodged within the last twenty years; in 1890 by the United States, and in 1897 by Germany. In 1898 the United States produced 26·2 per cent. of the world's iron output; Germany and Luxembourg, 21·6 per cent.; and the United Kingdom, 19·3 per cent. Since then the output of the United States has advanced to 42 per cent. of the world's production, and that of Germany to 22 per cent., while that of Great Britain has fallen to 15½ per cent. These figures show how rapid and considerable are the changes that are taking place from year to year in the relative international conditions of the iron industry.

The absolute and relative importance of each iron-producing district in the supply of home ores is indicated by the figures contained in the following table :—

SUMMARY OF OUTPUT OF IRON ORE IN EACH
BRITISH IRON-PRODUCING DISTRICT

DISTRICTS OR COUNTIES.	TOTAL.	PERCENTAGE OF THE TOTAL OUTPUT.
	Tons.	
1. Scotland	828,314	6·2
2. Cumberland and Lancashire	1,569,353	11·7
3. Yorkshire, N. Riding (Cleveland)	5,401,932	40·2
4. Staffordshire	815,379	6·1
5. Lincolnshire	1,843,926	13·7
6. Northamptonshire	1,751,427	13·0
7. Other counties	1,133,911	8·5
8. Ireland	81,762	·6
Total	13,426,004	100·0

According to Home Office returns the total quantity of iron ore available for furnaces in the United Kingdom in

1902, exclusive of mill and forge cinders, was 20,305,369 tons. This total is made up as follows :—

AVAILABLE IRON ORE IN 1902

	Tons.
British home output	13,426,004
Foreign ore imported (excluding "purple ore") . .	6,439,757
Purple ore imported	458,377
Gross total	20,324,138
Deduct exports	18,769
Net total	20,305,369

In the above table the purple ore has been calculated at 75 per cent. of the total raw cupreous iron pyrites imported, which amounted to 611,000 tons in 1902.

The comparative cost of extraction of iron ores is only one of many considerations that enter into their ultimate value. The character and richness of the ore, its chemical composition and physical properties, its distance from fuel and from centres of production, and its relation to the total cost of the assemblage of materials, are all relatively important matters. Taking the figures as they stand, the costs of extraction, subject to these qualifying circumstances, will run approximately as follows :—

GREAT BRITAIN.

	s.	d.		s.	d.
Scotland . .	3	6	to	4	6
Cleveland . .	2	0	,,	3	0
West Cumberland .	5	0	,,	8	0
Lincolnshire . .	1	6	,,	2	6
Northamptonshire .	1	3	,,	1	9

UNITED STATES.

	s.	d.		s.	d.
Mesabi . .	0	8	,,	1	3
Marquette .	2	6	,,	5	0
Gogebic . .	2	6	,,	3	6
Alabama .	1	6	,,	3	6
Cornwall .	2	6	,,	4	0

GERMANY.

	s.	d.		s.	d.
Lorraine . .	1	3	to	1	9
Luxembourg . .	1	3	,,	1	9
Spathic . . .	3	6	,,	4	0
Other ores (average)	4	0			

BELGIUM.

	s.	d.		s.	d.
Home ores[1] . .	4	0	,,	5	0
Luxembourg . .	1	3	,,	1	9

CANADA.

	s.	d.		s.	d.
Cape Breton . .	2	0	,,	5	0
Newfoundland .	2	0	,,	2	6

[1] Belgium mainly uses Luxembourg ores.

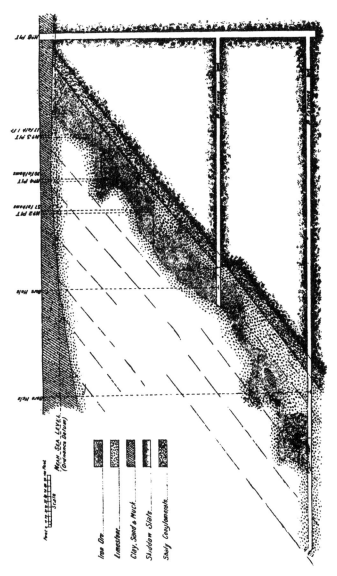

SECTION OF IRON ORE IN CUMBERLAND MINES

The differences in the cost of extracting iron ores are not so much due to wages as to physical conditions and methods of working. Speaking generally, miners are paid about 1s. per day more in this country than in Germany, and 1s. 2d. per day more than in France, while in the United States they are about, or nearly, 1s. per day more than here.

If the engineers of this country were as ready to accept basic steel as those of the Continent, it might be possible to greatly diminish our dependence on imported ores. I am aware of numerous iron ore deposits in this country that could, in that event, be much more fully utilised than they are at present.

As it is, however, our home supplies of hematite, or non-phosphoric ores, have lately been diminishing, so that if the British demand for acid steel is maintained, as it has hitherto been, we are likely to have to import increasing quantities of such ores. Within the last twenty years our home supplies of non-phosphoric ores have been reduced by nearly a million tons annually, owing to the declining supplies furnished by the mines of West Cumberland and North-west Lancashire. Explorations are going on by the Barrow Hematite Steel Company—of which the Duke of Devonshire is chairman—and other firms on the West Coast, with a view to finding other supplies in that region, but hitherto without much success. At the same time it is the opinion of some authorities that there is a great deal of ore still to be found in that district.

The immediate effect of this decline of iron ore output on the West Coast has been to develop in the West Cumberland district a large and increasing importation of foreign ores. Indeed, the West Coast generally now imports almost as much ore as it produces, in order to keep up its output of hematite, or non-phosphoric pig iron, known in the United States as Bessemer pig.

The same thing is happening, *mutatis mutandis*, in other districts. As a notable example of the change, I may mention the case of Scotland, which used only home ores about twenty years ago, but which last year imported nearly 2,000,000 tons of foreign ores, and has reduced its home output of iron ore from 3,500,000 tons in 1870 to less than 700,000 tons in 1903, partly because of the exhaustion of home supplies, and partly because of the demand for hematite pig iron, which home ores have not been suited to meet. Cleveland is another case of the same sort. In that district, practically all the iron produced twenty years ago was made from home ores, whereas in 1902 more than 2,000,000 tons of foreign ores were imported for the purpose of producing hematite iron. Finally, South Wales, which produced over half a million tons of iron ore in 1870, now produces practically no such ore, but used only foreign ores in 1902 to the extent of over 1,300,000 tons.

It will be seen, therefore, that under existing conditions the discontinuance of British iron ore imports would practically close some two-thirds of the ironworks in Scotland, all the ironworks in South Wales, nearly one-half of the ironworks in Cleveland, and nearly one-half of the blast furnaces in West Cumberland and North-west Lancashire. It would mean the reduction of the annual output of hematite iron in the country by about $3\frac{1}{2}$ million tons and would withdraw pig iron to that extent from the service of our great acid-steel industry, which, in its turn, would seriously react on the British supplies of steel specially suited and applied to the building of ships, and the manufacture of tyres, axles, wheels, and other important railway requirements.

The ore supplies of the future are a matter of much concern to the British iron trade. In Great Britain itself there is not much likelihood of new fields of any importance being discovered. The principal deposits in all districts alike have been pretty well proved. The Cleveland district, the main source of home supplies, has not increased its output for a number of years past; but whether this is a result of the exhaustion and limited character of the best supplies, or whether it is due to the increased demand for acid steel, which can only be produced from non-phosphoric ores, is a moot question. In most districts the supplies are more or less stationary, where they are not decreasing. There has been an increase of output in the ore-fields of the regions round about Frodingham, Wellingbro', Stoke-on-Trent, and one or two other places; but, on the other hand, the supplies of South Staffordshire, South Wales, South and West Yorkshire, Durham and Northumberland, and Scotland, have largely fallen off. This, unfortunately, is also the case with West Cumberland and North-west Lancashire, the only districts that yield ore of a pure and high quality in the British Islands. In every other district except these two the ores worked are only suited to the production of a more or less impure pig iron. This iron, nevertheless, is not, for that reason, unsuited to the manufacture of high-class steel. On the contrary, more than three-fourths, or approximately six million tons a year, of the steel output of Germany and a full third of the steel output of France are produced from phosphoric ores, and the use of such ores is greatly increasing in the United States, Belgium, Russia, and other countries.

FUEL SUPPLIES

The great bulk of the pig iron produced in Great Britain is made with coke fuel, but raw coal is used in Scotland and in some parts of the Midlands, including North Staffordshire, Notts, and Leicester. The total production of coke in Great Britain is computed at over

c

11,000,000 tons, of which nearly one-half is produced in Durham. This district supplies the whole of the coke used in the Cleveland iron industry and a large part of that required for the West Coast furnaces as well. The coking coal of Durham is of limited extent, and it is computed that it will not be able to maintain the present rate of consumption for more than sixty years. The other principal coke-producing districts are South and West Yorkshire, South Wales, and Lancashire. In these regions the coke supply is likely to have a materially longer life, which, however, has not been, and probably in the nature of the case cannot be, exactly determined. For at least half a century to come, the coke supply of Great Britain would seem to be pretty well assured, and that without necessarily adding materially to the cost of the product. Indeed, there is a probability that the actual production of the coke supply of the near future should be cheaper than that of the immediate past, inasmuch as by-product ovens are being more extensively employed than hitherto.

This would seem to be the natural and proper place to intimate that for a long period there was a general impression in this country that the use of by-product ovens tended to produce an inferior quality of coke, and hence the progress of such ovens, both in Great Britain and in some other countries—notably the United States—was extremely slow. It is doubtful whether 20 per cent. of our total coke supply is yet produced in such ovens, the great bulk of the ovens still employed being of the beehive type. And yet the by-product ovens give an average of about 75 per cent. of coke per 100 tons of coal against only about 66 per cent. yielded by the beehive, while the value of the by-products is variously computed at 3s. to 3s. 8d. per ton of coke produced, which value, in the case of the beehive, is not realisable, owing to the character of the plant and process employed.

NORTH-EASTERN STEEL COMPANY'S BYE-PRODUCT OVENS AND COKE CARS

The prejudice or objection against by-product coke has largely disappeared within recent years, and by-product plants are now being much more generally adopted by the leading coke-makers and coke-users throughout the country. This movement is tending to reduce the cost of coke. The practice now adopted on Tees-side is to coke in the vicinity of the blast furnaces instead of at the collieries. In this way the initial heat of the coking ovens is to a large extent retained and utilised, and other advantages are gained. Indeed, it has been found that coal can be carried from Durham to Tees-side, converted into coke there alongside the blast furnaces, and the whole cost involved, after making allowance for the by-products realised, is not more than 10s. per ton of coke, including everything; whereas the average selling price of blast-furnace coke on Tees-side was 26s. in 1900, 16s. in 1901, and 15s. 6d. in 1902. This compares not unfavourably with the average cost over the last ten years of Connellsville coke at ovens, which was about 8s. per ton, with a freight charge of 2s. to 3s. per ton to blast furnaces in the Pittsburg district.[1]

My friend Mr. Charles Kirchhoff, of New York, has summed up the situation in Cleveland in the following admirable statement :—

" The quantity of coal remaining in the Durham coal field is enormous, but up to the present only a comparatively limited area has been found to contain coal suitable for making a hard, tough, dense coke, suitable for blast furnace purposes, and these qualities are becoming more and more important as the blast furnace practice improves with greater heats and increased blast. It is possible that means may be found for making a good coke out of the small from the household and gas coal collieries, but unless this can be done we must be dependent on the

---

[1] American coke prices show considerable extremes, ranging over this period from 7s. 6d. to 12s. 6d. per ton at ovens in these ten years.

coking coal collieries. There are some coking collieries which have only recently been opened out, and will be able to work for many years chiefly, if not entirely, from the main coal seams, but we are already dependent for a part of our supplies of coke on collieries working only the thinner seams. There is sufficient coal in these to last for many years, but even in collieries where we are at present working partly from the main seams, we must become, as time goes on, gradually dependent on the thin seams. In considering the question of cost of the thin seams it has to be borne in mind that not only is the coal costly to hew, but also that it requires additional cleaning when brought to bank, and does not, as a rule, make quite as good coke after everything has been done to improve it as the thicker seams. Limestone, the other chief material used for making iron, is available in vast quantities, and in various districts."

CHAPTER III

THE IRONMAKING DISTRICTS OF GREAT BRITAIN

GREAT BRITAIN has altogether nineteen pig-iron-making districts, of which, in 1903, two produced over a million tons each, four between 500,000 and a million tons each, seven between 200,000 tons and half a million tons each, and the remainder less than 100,000 tons each.

The two leading districts are those of Cleveland and Scotland, the former producing about two million tons annually and the latter about 1,300,000 tons. In both districts, hematite pig iron is produced to the extent of 600,000 to 700,000 tons annually from imported ores, in addition to the considerable quantities still annually produced from local ores. In Scotland, the local ores have within the last twenty years largely and rapidly declined, until from an annual supply of 2½ million tons, the present rate of domestic output does not much exceed one-fifth of that quantity. In Cleveland the highest annual ore output hitherto attained has been about 6½ million tons, but the output over the last few years has averaged about a million tons under that figure.

Of the other ironmaking districts, West Cumberland, Lancashire, and South Wales are almost entirely engaged in producing hematite or Bessemer iron, in the two former regions partly with domestic and partly with imported ores, and in the latter district with imported ores only.

The rest of British ironmaking centres use local ore only, and produce only forge and foundry or basic pig iron. The latter description of iron has only been produced since the year 1880, and the present rate of output is about a million tons a year, in eleven different districts, of which Cumberland is the most important.

The proportions of different descriptions of pig iron produced in Great Britain are about as under :—

Forge and foundry	.	.	44	per cent.
Hematite	.	.	40	,,
Basic iron	.	.	11	,,
Other descriptions	.	.	5	,,

SCOTLAND

THE RAW MATERIALS USED IN THE SCOTCH IRON INDUSTRY

There is little of a novel or advanced kind, with an exception here and there, to be found in the smelting practice of the Scottish ironmasters, for, experiencing the good fortune to meet the ironstone fuel and flux in the same mines, and erecting their blast furnaces actually at the pit's mouth, that is to say, directly upon the carboniferous strata, they have been surrounded with a set of conditions, the immediate effect of which was to keep at a low standard the first items of cost of production, so that the necessity has not here been felt for that attention to economy in fuel which has presented itself in other less favoured localities, where the ore is often poor and the fuel has to be brought from a distance. Yet whilst the Scottish ironmasters have been so favourably situated in the past with respect to the raw materials, now in some cases the conditions are altered ; the pits in the neighbourhood of some of the furnaces becoming exhausted, the materials have to be brought from a distance.

The local iron-producing materials are obtained over a comparatively small area, chiefly within and bordering on the valleys of the Clyde and Forth, and they are principally found in Lanarkshire, Ayrshire being second in this respect. The other counties comprised within the coal and iron-stone-yielding area are Renfrewshire and Dumbartonshire in the vale of Clyde, and Stirlingshire, Fife, Clackmannan, Kinross, East Lothian, Midlothian, and Linlithgowshire or West Lothian in the vale of the Forth. The blast furnaces of Scotland are, with one exception, all situated within this area. Thus the iron district may be said to extend from the Firth of Forth a little to the east of Edinburgh to the opposite point on the west coast, and to some distance south of this line.

This mineral district is about eighty miles in length, forty miles in extreme breadth, and 1,500 yards deep. It is most fully developed in Lanarkshire, in which county, according to the Royal Commissioners' Report for 1871, there was then contained over 2,000 million tons of coal. In the valley of the Clyde alone there were then computed to be 900 millions of tons within 1,060 feet of the surface. The pits through which the minerals are raised vary from 30 to 180 fathoms in depth, and as a rule are not heavily watered.

Coal.—The blast furnaces of Lanarkshire and Ayrshire have now been at regular work for over a century, and during three-quarters of that time they have worked mainly on the coal from two or three not exceptionally thick seams; add to this that until the last fifteen or twenty years both mining and smelting were conducted in the most wasteful manner, and it will be no cause for surprise that the best splint coals are showing signs of exhaustion. Mining engineers have variously estimated the time for the exhaustion of the good splint coals of Lanarkshire at from ten to twenty years, and already the scarcity is making itself felt by those works which depend on the open market for their fuel supplies. To meet this scarcity of splint coal, some works are endeavouring to use in its place the softer semi-splint coals, with results which, so far, do not conduce to the comfort of their furnace managers. A more promising plan has been tried by one large firm, who coke the coal from the lower seams in very fine by-product ovens, and use a small proportion of coke with each barrow of coal.

With the exception of two firms, who use from 10 to 25 per cent. coke, all the Scotch furnaces now work with raw coal.

Blackband.—The Lanarkshire blackband, which was discovered in 1801, has been practically exhausted. There are now no pits in the Lanarkshire coal-fields working it as a principal product, though a small quantity of a thin blackband is raised with the gas coal at one or two pits. Some blackband of excellent quality is still raised in Fife and Midlothian for smelting in the Lanarkshire furnaces, and the somewhat leaner blackbands of Ayrshire are still fairly plentiful.

Clayband.—From somewhat different causes, the use of clayband ores has also declined greatly, and these are now but little worked, except in cases where they can be worked with a coal seam. The greatly increased cost of mining labour is partly responsible for this, whilst the greater attention paid to sampling and chemical analysis since hematite smelting became general has shown the necessity of abandoning many pits working poor ores.

Other Ores.—Hardly any iron ore is at present worked in Scotland except the bedded claybands and blackbands of the carboniferous system, though several small vein deposits of hematite are known to exist in the older rocks, and comparatively small quantities have been worked from time to time; consequently the importation of foreign ores, which was almost unknown twenty years ago, has been steadily growing year by year for the last quarter of a century. This movement appears likely to continue.

Blast Furnace Equipment and Practice.—There is a greater uniformity in both dimensions and output of the furnaces at different works in Scotland than in any other district. In 1872 the average make per furnace per week was 165 tons, with a consumption of 2·95 tons of coal per ton of pig. In 1884 the production had increased to 200 tons, and the coal was reduced to 2·20 tons. In 1889 the production had increased to 270 tons, and the coal consumption decreased to 1·83 tons. The average weekly production is now 265 to 300 tons. The coal consumed per ton shows a fractional increase—poorer results being due entirely to the inferior quality of coal and ores used.

To those accustomed to the hard driving of some recently constructed coke furnaces, Scotch blast furnace makes will appear small ; it should not, however, be too hastily concluded that the proprietors and their managers are ignorant of their business. A furnace working on splint coal has to combine in itself a coke oven and a blast furnace, and if it is driven so fast that any of the coal reaches the zone of fusion without having its 35 or 40 per cent. of water and volatile hydrocarbons expelled, the temperature there is so reduced as to completely disorganise the working. An obvious remedy would appear to be an increase in the height of the furnaces, and this was tried, and gave very good results so long as uniformly hard coal was used.

As almost all the Scotch works are now equipped with by-product plants, the manager has to work with one eye on this department, and anything which tends to produce irregular driving in the furnace is very quickly reflected on the returns from the chemical department. The quantity of sulphate of ammonia obtained from smelting pig iron in Scotch furnaces ranges from 17,000 to 18,000 tons annually. The value of the by-products is computed at about 5s. per ton of pig made.

In one respect—the value of an increased number of tuyeres—Scotch practice has anticipated the conclusions of modern designers. For many years past eight or nine tuyeres have been the rule in Scotland, and in the last few years several have been built with twelve.

All the works in Scotland are now fitted with a full equipment of firebrick stoves, and fairly high temperatures (1,200° to 1,400° F.) are the rule. The stove which has found most favour is the Ford Moncur—nine or ten out of the sixteen working plants in Scotland being fitted with this type, and some of the stoves have now been at work over ten years without any repairs other than the renewal of hot-blast valves.

With the comparatively small makes in vogue there has been no opening for blowing engines or charging machinery of the American type, but pig lifting and breaking machinery has been introduced at Messrs. Dixon's two works, Govan and Calder, and is giving complete satisfaction.

FINISHED IRON.—At the present time there are employed in the manufacture of malleable iron in Scotland 22 firms, owning 25 works, consisting of 396 puddling furnaces, 38 scrap furnaces, 17 bar mills, 23 guide mills, 8 strip mills, 21 sheet mills, producing 325,000 tons per annum finished iron of all kinds. All the works, with one or two exceptions, are situated in the Coatbridge and Motherwell districts of Lanarkshire.

No new process having been introduced in the manufacture of puddled iron, the fundamental principles are just the same as have been in operation for the last fifty years or more; so that the only means of lowering the costs in order to meet the keen competition of modern times is by adopting from time to time all the minor improvements in furnaces and machinery, whereby the waste of material and consumption of fuel are lessened, the output increased, and thus the best results are obtained from the plant, and the general wages and charges are reduced. In this respect the various works have not been slow in adopting any means which they considered would be a benefit to them in their respective branches.

THE OPEN-HEARTH STEEL INDUSTRY.—This is at once one of the most recent and one of the most strikingly progressive of the many leading industries of Scotland. So recently as 1876 no steel shipbuilding tonnage at all was constructed in Great Britain, but five years later the tonnage built in steel had increased to 71,000 tons, and by 1893 steel manufacturers had practically got the field all to themselves, and built 637 vessels of 1,158,000 tons, while the tonnage of iron ships had fallen to 36,000. In 1900 nearly two million tons of new shipping were built in steel.

This was the most important economic movement in the history of the open-hearth steel industry, and in the progress and ultimate success of that movement the West of Scotland bore an honourable and conspicuous part. Especially was this the case with the Steel Company of Scotland, which more or less paved the way and made things easy for the numerous steel-manufacturing companies that followed. The many problems that had to be solved before this new description of steel could either be manufactured so as to answer all the requirements of Lloyd's, the Admiralty, and structural engineers, or applied on a large scale with confidence, were all more or less worked out at these works, and not in shipbuilding alone, but in the manufacture of steel suited to such various and important structures as the Forth Bridge, locomotive boilers and fire-boxes, marine appliances, forgings and castings of all kinds, and numerous other uses.

From 1880 the development of the open-hearth steel industry in Scotland has been rapid and remarkable. Not only has the number of furnaces advanced from about a dozen to over 130, and the quantity produced from 60,000 to nearly a million tons, but the progress made in cheapening the cost of production, in getting out much larger quantities with a given plant, and in successful competition with iron for structural purposes, has marked an important era in metallurgical practice. Only a few years ago the average annual output of open-hearth steel was not more than 4,000 tons per furnace, whereas at some of the most modern works in Scotland it is now over 14,000 tons a year, or about the same as the average annual output from the Scotch blast furnaces.

CLEVELAND

In the *History of Cleveland*, Graves speaks of four farm-houses at Middlesbrough about three-quarters of a century ago. In 1829 the Middlesbrough Estate Owners Company was formed for the purchase of the land that now bears the name of that town. In 1831 the town of Middlesbrough had a population of 134. In 1850 the population had grown to over 6,000. In 1846 Bolckow and Vaughan started their ironworks at Witton Park. In 1850 there were thirty-eight blast furnaces in the north of England, mostly owned in Durham, by the Weardale and Derwent Companies, who depended mainly on the ores of the coal measures, which yielded 36 per cent. of iron.

The ironstone of the Cleveland district was first worked in a systematic way at Grosmont, near Whitby. It is found in two seams or bands, known as the Pecten and the Avicula. The former consists of 3 feet of ironstone, divided in the middle by a bed of shale of 1½ feet thick. Separated from this by 30 feet or more of shale is the other seam, the Avicula, embracing 4½ feet of ironstone, besides 2 feet of shale ; and it is by these two bands uniting, as well as increasing in thickness, that we have farther north the Main Cleveland Seam, as it is termed. In the northern portion of the field considerable irregularity in character is also observable. At Codhill, out of a considerable depth of ironstone, interspersed with shale beds, only a 5½-feet working is pursued ; and this, in consequence of more or less shale bands running through the ironstone itself, only yields about 28 per cent. of metal. A little to the east of Codhill are the Belmont Mines, where the shales have thinned out, and in consequence the yield of iron is about 30 per cent., the seam at the same time having increased in height to 7¼ feet. At Skelton, still further east, a marked improvement, both in thickness and in quality, is again discernible. The north side of the vale of Guisbro' is formed of an elevated ridge of land, separating this valley from that of the Tees. At the western edge of this ridge are the Normanby Mines, where the stone is worked at an average thickness of about 8 feet, and containing 31½ per cent. of iron. There is a general dip of the seam to the east from this point, and in its progress in that direction there is a gradual increase in thickness, and a little improvement in percentage of iron. It continues in this way past Eston and Upleatham, until it reaches Rockliffe, where it attains a thickness of nearly 18 feet, after which it splits again into bands, and, as far as is known, resumes towards the east and south the character formerly observed as attaching to it at Grosmont, near Whitby. From this district the output of ironstone up to the year 1854 did not exceed half a million tons.

Conditions and Cost of Production in Cleveland.—The

cost of producing iron, as of practically all commodities, is made up mainly of wages, but, to a larger extent than most other commodities, iron and steel have to face the heavy charges incidental to royalties, transport, and stores. Some years ago an estimate was made by Mr. Hugh Bell, of the Clarence Ironworks, Middlesbrough, which throws a good deal of valuable light on the problem just stated. That gentleman found that the total normal cost of producing a million tons of pig iron on Tees-side, during a period of five years, was £2,073,558, made up in the following proportions, which have here been calculated in percentages of the total amount:—

			£		Per cent. of Total.
Wages	.	.	963,048	...	46·4
Salaries	.	.	57,075	...	2·7
Railway dues	.	.	468,973	...	22·6
Stores	.	.	303,773	...	14·6
Royalties	.	.	178,163	...	8·5
Establishment	.	.	42,824	...	2·1
Rates, etc.	.	.	38,400	...	1·8
Sundries	.	.	21,320	...	1·0
Total		£2,073,558			99·7

These figures make it clear that wages is the greatest of all the items to be reckoned with, and that in normal times the cost of labour represented 46·4 per cent. of the whole outlay.

When the costs of producing iron in Great Britain had risen materially above the average of the five years to which Mr. Bell's figures applied, I attempted an analysis of the differences in the several items tabulated, due to different conditions of trade, and I found that at that time the cost of railway transport was 13 per cent. more than the standard or normal rates, which means that the particular firm to which these figures apply would be paying in respect of the transport of practically the same traffic, about £61,000 more than it paid when trade was not so good. The item of stores stands for 14·6 per cent. of the total cost of producing pig iron, and this figure was also certain to have been largely increased. If stores generally advanced *pari passu* with the advance in iron and steel, they would have mounted to a figure at least 50 per cent. above normal rates, which means that instead of being £303,773, they would have increased by £152,000, and would not be less than £456,000. Royalties, which stand for 8·5 per cent. of the total sum, were not likely to be very different unless there should happen to be, in regard to any of them, the unusual arrangement that royalty rents should rise or fall with the prices of coal, pig iron, or some kindred commodity. The item of rates, which is returned at 1·87 per cent. of the total cost of production, or about 9*d.* per ton, was not likely to have absolutely fallen. Finally, the items of salaries (2·7 per cent.), establishment (2·1 per cent.), and sundries (1·0 per cent.), make up unitedly about £121,000, or nearly half a crown per ton of pig produced. It would be unreasonable to suppose that the three heads which make up this figure have remained unvaried, while other charges have advanced all round. It is more than probable that salaries and establishment charges, like wages, had increased; in the absence of a clue to the amount of the increase, the hypothetical figure of 20 per cent. advance, or £24,000 for the three items tabulated, may be assumed.

FINISHED IRON.—A quarter of a century ago the Cleveland district was the principal centre of the finished iron industry of Great Britain, the output in some years approaching 900,000 tons a year. Of late years this industry has declined, and the output is not now 150,000 tons annually. There are still 275 puddling furnaces in the district, out of a total of 1,528 left standing in the country as a whole. The products of this branch of industry are chiefly bars, ship-plates, rounds and squares, angles, and sheets.

THE STEEL INDUSTRY.—For ten years past the steel industry of Cleveland has been running an almost neck-to-neck race with that of Scotland, so far as open-hearth steel is concerned, and now the one district, and then the other, takes the lead. But Cleveland has also two important works engaged in the manufacture of Bessemer steel, while Scotland has only one. Both districts are mainly engaged in producing ship-plates and angles, the one for the Clyde, and the other for the Wear, Tyne, Tees, and the Hartlepools. The three latter localities, it may be added, now produce a considerably larger tonnage of shipbuilding than the Clyde. In three years out of the last five, the tonnage of open-hearth steel turned out in the North of England has exceeded a million tons, while the output of Bessemer steel ingots varies between 350,000 and 400,000 tons a year, almost wholly of the basic variety. The Scotch and North of England steelworks carry on the steel industry under more or less parallel conditions as to costs and prices.

THE NORTH-WEST COAST

This designation is usually given to the ironmaking districts of West Cumberland and North-west Lancashire, a region which embraces eighty-one blast furnaces, four important steel plants, produces annually 1,500,000 to 1,600,000 tons of pig iron, raises well on to $1\frac{3}{4}$ million tons of iron ore, and turns out 750,000 to 800,000 tons of Bessemer and open-hearth steel.

This district has produced iron from almost prehistoric times. Its modern history may be said to begin from 1865, when the Barrow Hematite Steel Company built Bessemer works, capable of producing 2,000 tons of steel weekly, from eighteen converters, being then by far the largest steelworks in the world. Indeed, the capacity of the Barrow works at that time exceeded the total steel production of the world only ten years before.

In those days, it was believed that the resources of the North-west Coast were practically unlimited. No other district then produced non-phosphoric ores on a scale of any importance. The output of these ores rose to a maximum of over 2½ million tons annually. Some of the best deposits have, however, since been largely exhausted, and as few new deposits of any magnitude have been found, the output of iron ore has declined to such an extent that the district now requires to import nearly one-half of its annual requirements.

Raw Materials.—While the West Coast works have probably quite as cheap supplies of non-phosphoric iron ore at their command, as any other district, they are not so well situated in respect of coal and coke. West Cumberland has, it is true, a small coal-field of its own, but the coal is inferior, relatively dear to work, and does not, as a rule, produce a satisfactory coke. Hence, the bulk of the fuel required is brought into the district from either South Durham or the Yorkshire coal-field, at a freight rate of 6s. to 7s. 6d. per ton, against 2s. to 2s. 6d. per ton, and even less, paid by the ironmasters of Cleveland and Scotland.

Steel.—Unlike all the other ironmaking regions of Great Britain, the West Coast produces only hematite iron and spiegeleisen, but in Lancashire there is an important plant at Wigan that produces a limited quantity of basic iron, as well as hematite and spiegeleisen. The output of Bessemer steel on the West Coast now exceeds that of any other district in Great Britain, produced by three important works. The output of open-hearth steel is exceeded by that of four other districts. The principal finished product is rails. The make of basic steel is *nil.*

D

SOUTH WALES

About twenty-seven years ago this district shared, with that of Cleveland, the distinction of producing more finished iron in the form of rails, bars, and plates, than any other. To-day the output of such iron is almost *nil*. The output of puddled iron, in fact, has fallen from over 800,000 tons to less than 10,000 tons annually. While this movement has been in progress, the manufacture of steel has advanced to well over a million tons. Indeed, in the early days of the Bessemer process, South Wales became the most extensive steel-producing district in the world, having no fewer than six large plants in regular operation.[1] Those have since been reduced to three, and there is, in addition, a small plant of a special character, near Newport. The reduction in the number of operative works is due to the development of steel-rail making plants in other home districts and abroad, and to the encroachments of the open-hearth process.

This district has also important historical claims. It has been the cradle and the continuous home of the tin-plate industry. It was the first to test the merits of the Bessemer process, and to build works to carry it on upon a large scale. It built at Landore the first commercial plant designed to carry on the open-hearth process. It is associated with the historic names and mechanical and metallurgical achievements of Cort, Rogers, Abraham Darby, Crawshay, Guest, and others, and it was at Blaenavon works that the practicability of the basic process was demonstrated by its discoverers—first on a laboratory scale, and afterwards as an everyday business.

Natural Resources.—Nevertheless, South Wales has not natural resources of the first order. Its coal, which is

[1] Those were Dowlais, Blaenavon, Tredegar, Ebbw Vale, Rhymney, and Cyfarthfa.

chiefly suited for steaming purposes, is more costly than that of most other British fields. Its iron ores, always relatively costly, have now been almost entirely superseded by imported materials from Spain and elsewhere. It is mountainous, and most of the important works are situated at elevations which render railway transport relatively expensive. It is more or less like the fly in amber which led the *savants* to wonder how it got there.

Past and Present.—There are, however, an old Wales and a new. The old Wales consisted of very small blast furnaces, producing 4,000 to 5,000 tons of pig iron annually, and built so strongly that they seemed destined to resist even the crack of doom;[1] of a multitude of small forges producing bars for the tin-plate industry, or rails for our earlier railway lines by the strenuous labour of the puddling process; of iron mines that did well if they yielded a 35 per cent. ore at 12s. per ton at the rate of 25,000 to 40,000 tons a year; of a labour community that understood no English, and was as much isolated from the rest of the British Isles in ideas, habits, and traditions, as if they had lived in Fiji; of canal transportation that was slow and imperfect in many ways; and of limited and highly inefficient dock accommodation.

The new Wales consists of blast-furnace plants that produce as much pig iron per unit in a month as the old furnaces did in twelve; of ores entirely imported from abroad; of a collapsed and practically moribund finished iron industry; of a steel output exceeding a million tons of ingots annually from about thirty-five different works; of a tin-plate industry that practically supplies all other lands with that product, excepting only the United States: while Welsh managers and Welsh workmen have gone out into all the world and preached the gospel of sound

[1] I saw some of these furnaces still standing at Dowlais and Cyfarthfa only four or five years ago.

and advanced practical metallurgy to every community, whereby many of them that believed have been saved. The shipping ports and railway facilities of Wales to-day are not excelled by any.

The ironmaking plants of South Wales consist of fifty-five blast furnaces, of which some twenty-one were in blast in 1903, while only about a dozen puddling furnaces are left out of more than five hundred in the palmy days of that industry. The steel-manufacturing plants consist of nearly a hundred open-hearth furnaces and twelve Bessemer converters, capable of producing nearly two million tons of steel annually, but hitherto producing only from a million to a million and a quarter tons annually.

The principal products of the steelworks of South Wales are rails and tin-plate bars. Of the latter the output is over 450,000 tons a year; of the former the production varies from 150,000 tons to 230,000 tons. Until a year or two ago this district produced only acid steel. It now produces both acid and basic steel, to the extent of about 700,000 tons by the open hearth, and 350,000 tons by the Bessemer process.

OTHER DISTRICTS

The districts so far dealt with are all more or less on the seaboard. We now come to consider a group of inland districts that are all more or less remote from the sea. These districts embrace North and South Staffordshire, Derbyshire, Lincolnshire, Northamptonshire, Notts, Leicestershire, South and West Yorkshire, and Shropshire. In these districts there are altogether 203 blast furnaces, or 36 per cent. of the total of the kingdom, while the annual production of pig iron is from two to two and a quarter million tons, by far the largest bulk of which is used in supplying the home markets. Excepting about 600,000 tons of basic iron, the products of these districts are almost entirely forge and foundry iron, which feed the forges of South Staffordshire, South and West Yorkshire, and Shropshire, and the foundries of the West Riding of Yorkshire and the Midlands generally.

The smelting practice of this region is generally behind that of the other regions named, and hence it is not entirely a matter of surprise that while the average annual output per furnace in Great Britain is about 26,000 tons, and about 30,000 tons if these districts are disregarded, the average of the Midland furnaces does not exceed 18,000 tons, and some of them fall to little more than 15,000 tons. This result is largely attributable to having to deal with a lean, if generally cheap ore, and to a less satis- factory coke than is usually at the command of the North-east and North-west smelters. Much of this iron is also produced with raw coal fuel, in which cases the blast furnace has to perform the functions of a coke oven as well. Lincolnshire, Northamptonshire, and Notts pro- duce remarkably cheap iron in the best plants, the ores costing but little over 2s. per ton at the mines, and averaging perhaps 30 per cent. of iron. The business, however, is not uniformly satisfactory, and in 1902, which was a fairly good business period, only about 60 per cent. of all the available furnaces in the Midland districts were in blast. The largest individual producer in these districts was South Staffordshire, which ranges between 365,000 and 400,000 tons of pig iron annually, followed by Derby- shire with 320,000 tons, and Lincolnshire with 310,000 tons in 1902.

South Staffordshire has always enjoyed the distinction of leading in the manufacture of finished iron, and of having largely thereby created the "Black Country." At one time the region produced about a million tons of finished iron annually, and had over a thousand puddling furnaces in operation. This output has now declined to about 230,000 tons annually, and 260 furnaces; but even so, Staffordshire continues to lead. None of the other inland districts, except South and West Yorkshire produce finished iron on a material scale.

The last-named districts only produce about 264,000 tons of pig iron annually, but they turn out about half a million tons of Bessemer and open-hearth steel annually, in addition to the considerable quantity of crucible steel produced in and around Sheffield.

The steel of this locality is mainly used for special purposes, such as castings, forgings, armour plates, projectiles, wheels, axles, tyres, cutlery, and kindred wants. Steel rails, and blooms and billets, are also made to a considerable extent.

South Staffordshire produces about 200,000 tons of open-hearth steel and over 100,000 tons of Bessemer steel, in lieu of the million tons of puddled iron that it formerly produced, so that from a quantitative point of view this district has declined,—being almost the only one in the kingdom that has done so. This result is due in part to the exhaustion of its raw material, and in part to the high cost of reaching the sea.

CHAPTER IV

BRITISH PIG-IRON-MAKING CONDITIONS

THE principal descriptions of pig iron produced in Great Britain are (1) forge and foundry, and (2) Bessemer or hematite iron. These two descriptions run pretty well on all fours from year to year. There is no record of the quantities of forge iron and of foundry iron as such, but there are still over a million tons of forge iron used in Great Britain alone in producing manufactured iron, and it is probable that at least half a million tons more are exported, which would make 40 per cent. of the total output of the two descriptions, and this would leave perhaps 60 per cent. of the combined total for foundry iron.

Hematite iron is only produced in six of the principal ironmaking districts of Great Britain, the more important being West Cumberland, South Wales, and Scotland. The total output of this description ranges from $3\frac{1}{2}$ to 4 million tons a year, and the percentage of home ores used in its production runs from 20 to 23 per cent. of the total supply, the rest being provided by Spain, Greece, and other countries, as already set forth.[1] The home hematite ores are exclusively raised and mainly consumed in West Cumberland and Lancashire.

Basic pig iron is now produced in eleven different centres of the trade. The largest output is in North

[1] *Op. cit.*, p. 11 *ante.*

Yorkshire, followed in the order of their importance by South and West Yorkshire and South Staffordshire. The total output is now more than a million tons a year. In 1904 basic iron was 14 per cent. of the total iron output of the kingdom. This is naturally regarded as a very inadequate relative output for a country whose ore resources are mostly phosphoric, and therefore unsuited to the production of iron for the acid steel process. The relative output of basic iron is, however, increasing from year to year, and is likely to continue to do so.

The only other description of British pig iron that requires to be named is that known as spiegeleisen, which is produced in five different ironmaking centres—namely, North Yorkshire, Lancashire, West Cumberland, South Wales, and North Wales. The annual output of spiegeleisen, ferro-manganese, and ferro-silicon, is 185,000 to 200,000 tons a year. These products are made entirely from imported ores, the main sources of supply being India, Russia, Chili, Turkey, and Brazil.

In 1850 the total production of pig iron throughout the world was under five million tons. Ten years later the output had advanced to 7,400,000 tons, in 1870 it was 11,900,000 tons, and in 1880 it was 18,484,000 tons. Between 1880 and 1890 there was an increase of $9\frac{1}{4}$ million tons, which compares with an increase of rather over $13\frac{3}{4}$ million tons in the previous thirty years. But between 1890 and 1900 the world's increased make of iron was close on $13\frac{1}{2}$ million tons, or almost as much as the amount of increase in the period 1850–1880.

Up to the year 1870 Great Britain produced one half or more of the total pig iron output of the world. For the period 1871–85, the British proportion was 43·9 per cent., that of the United States was 18·7 per cent., and that of Germany and Luxembourg was 15·4 per cent. For the period 1886–96, the British proportion was only 29·9 per cent., while that of the United States was 30·9 per cent., and that of Germany was 18·9 per cent. In the year 1903 Great Britain produced 20 per cent., the United States 42 per cent., and Germany 25½ per cent. The relative decline of British output in the last ten years has been very marked. We were second to the United States for the first time in 1890, and to Germany in 1902–3.

In this country blast furnaces still produce on an average less than 28,000 tons of pig iron per annum, whereas in the United States the average annual output of pig iron per furnace operated is more than double that quantity, and in the State of Pennsylvania the average annual output is not much under three times the British average. It may be, and probably is, the case that the conditions here do not admit of ever reaching the American figures. In Scotland, for example, where raw coal has to be used, because it is of the splint variety, that does not admit of coking, it has been taken for granted that it is not practicable to greatly exceed an output of 300 tons per furnace per week, and the same remark applies, *mutatis mutandis*, to the furnaces in some parts of the Midlands, including North Staffordshire. Nevertheless, there is much room for improvement, both in blast furnaces and in steelworks, and one of the best evidences of this fact that can be furnished is the limited use hitherto made of open-hearth charging machines, which are now all but universal in the United States.

The advantage of locating blast furnaces near the sea was early recognised, especially in the case of those installations whose raw material was supplied from abroad; nowadays, nearly all large plants seek such a position near a seaport, and thus avoid the costs of handling and transport which are incurred by inland works. The net cost of a ton of pig iron under these conditions, according to the calculations of the well-known German engineer

Herr Lürmann, can be reduced, by completely utilising the blast furnace gas, by about 6.88 francs. In some cases this reduction in cost may be as much as fifteen or sixteen francs.

The introduction of electric power is a great source of economy, and one could hardly mention a well-equipped blast furnace where electricity is not employed for power, for transmission, and for driving the auxiliary apparatus.

Some years ago the following figures were given as the approximate costs of conveying the material required to make one ton of pig iron in the leading ironmaking districts of this country :—

Middlesbrough . . . 8s. 6d. per ton of pig.		
South Wales . . . . 16s. 0d. ,, ,,		
Lincolnshire . . . . 12s. 6d. ,, ,,		
Lancashire . . . . 15s. 1d. ,, ,,		
Cumberland . . . . 14s. 8d. ,, ,,		
Scotland . . 6s. 8d. to 7s. 8d. ,, ,,		

To these charges have to be added the cost of reaching the seaboard or tide-water, which in the case of most of the above districts is probably not more than 1s. 6d. to 2s. 6d. per ton, but in the case of the Midlands reaches 10s. to 12s. 6d. If we had American transportation charges, the above costs would in all cases be very largely reduced, and the cost of reaching the seaboard or tide-water would not be by any means so serious a matter as it now is.

It need hardly be said that the relative as well as the absolute cost of the production of pig iron has much to do with the success of the industry of which that metal is the staple product. For that reason the following statement of approximate costs for the principal iron-producing nations is of interest, and not without commanding importance :—

APPROXIMATE COST OF PRODUCTION OF A TON OF PIG IRON IN VARIOUS COUNTRIES[1]

	Ore and Lime.	Fuel.	Total.	Wages.	Various Expenses.	Grand Total.
	£ s. d.	£ s. d.	£ s. d.	£ s. d.	£ s. d.	£ s. d.
Great Britain, Bessemer pig iron	1 7 0	0 11 0	1 18 0	0 2 9	0 2 0	2 2 9
Great Britain, pig iron, forge	0 17 0	0 11 11	1 8 11	0 2 10	0 1 6	1 13 3
Sweden, charcoal-smelted iron, Bessemer . .	1 11 2	1 9 11	3 1 1	0 4 5	0 5 0	3 10 6
Sweden, pig iron, forge .	1 3 3	1 5 8	2 8 11	0 3 5	0 4 7	2 16 11
United States America, charcoal-smelted iron .	0 16 6	1 13 9	2 10 3	0 7 5	0 4 7	3 2 3
United States, coke and anthracite . . .	1 12 10	0 12 11	2 5 9	0 6 1	0 3 0	2 14 10
On the Continent, pig iron, forge	0 17 5	0 16 11	1 14 4	0 2 2	0 0 11	1 17 5
On the Continent, basic iron	0 14 8	0 15 7	1 10 3	0 2 1	0 1 0	1 13 4
,, ,, various .	0 7 2	1 0 6	1 7 8	0 2 8	0 1 2	1 11 6

As the most important centre of the British iron industry is the Cleveland district in North Yorkshire, and as that district has much larger reserves of ironstone, and is almost nearer to large available supplies of good coke than any other, it is of importance to consider what its future is likely to be. Most of those who have written or spoken on the matter have an impression that the future of Cleveland is better assured than that of any other iron-making district in Europe. This is probable enough, but there is another side to the matter which should not be entirely overlooked. One who has every opportunity for mastering the facts of the case may be left to present this side.

Mr. A. F. Pease, of Darlington, in a communication made to the *Iron and Coal Trades Review*, in 1901, had the following remarks :—

[1] These figures are given on the authority of the Swedish Ironmasters' Association. In the majority of cases they are only approximately accurate as applied to the conditions of 1904.

" We have in Cleveland an iron ore, the best of which does not contain more than thirty-three per cent. of iron (dried at 212 degrees). This may be roughly divided into two distinct qualities.

" 1. 'Best' ironstone, which is worked from mines where the whole section of the main Cleveland ironstone seam is sent to the furnaces, and this stone will as a rule contain more than twenty-nine per cent. of iron (dried at 212 degrees).

" 2. 'Shale' ironstone, which is won from mines where the middle section of the seam contains so little iron and so much silica that it has to be cast back; and even after this has been done the remainder of the seam will not exceed 29 per cent. of iron, and in some cases considerably less.

" The supply of the best ironstone in Cleveland is limited; probably there does not remain more than from 60,000,000 to 70,000,000 tons.

" The supply of 'shale' ironstone is unlimited, the quality getting gradually poorer in a southerly direction. During the year 1900 there were twenty mines working in Cleveland, of which fourteen were working in best stone and six were working in shale, though the middle band had to be picked out in some districts of the mines included as working best stone. The output from the whole of the Cleveland mines was about 5,500,000 tons, of which about one-fifth would be won from the shale mines. If, therefore, we continue to exhaust the best mines at the present rate of rather more than 4,000,000 tons a year, their life will only be about seventeen years. This is not what will take place in actual practice, as in a few years' time, if it has not already begun, the output from the best mines will be reduced, and it will be many years longer before the last ton of best ironstone is worked."

Mr. Pease has assumed that for every four tons of ironstone brought to bank at a cost of 2s. 9d. per ton, one ton has to be thrown out, making the other three tons average 3s. 8d., and a further 3d. for royalty brings the cost per ton at mines up to 3s. 11d. He has also assumed the cost of coke at the ovens to be 11s. 2d. per ton, which would mean 13s. 3d. to 13s. 6d. at furnaces on Tees-side. He further computes the future cost of producing Cleveland iron at the following figures :—

	Per ton.		£	s.	d.
	s.	d.			
3½ tons ironstone (27 to 28 per cent. iron), at	3	11			
Dues to Middlesbrough . .	1	3			
	5	2	0	18	1
24 cwt. coke . . .	11	2			
Dues to Middlesbrough . .	2	3			
	13	5	0	16	1·20
⅜ ton limestone . . .	1	7			
Dues to Middlesbrough . .	2	3			
	3	10	0	2	6·66
Coals			0	1	0
			1	17	8·86
Furnace wages, charges, salaries, repairs, etc.			0	7	0
			£2	4	8·86

Mr. Pease reasons that if No. 3 Cleveland iron were 45s. 6d., the average price realised for all qualities would be less rather than more than 44s. 6d.

"We should, therefore, have a loss per ton of 2·86d., and this without allowing for any interest on capital, depreciation of plant, or for the sundry obligations as regards subscriptions, etc., which devolve on the coal owner, mine owner, and blast furnace owner."

The following table indicates the order of importance in point of volume of production of pig iron of each of the producing countries between 1880 and 1904 :—

1880.	1890.	1900.	1904.
Great Britain.	United States.	United States.	United States.
United States.	Great Britain.	Great Britain.	Germany.
Germany.	Germany.	Germany.	Great Britain.
France.	France.	Russia.	Russia.
Belgium.	Austria-Hungary.	France.	France.
Austria-Hungary.	Russia.	Austria-Hungary.	Austria-Hungary.
Russia.	Belgium.	Belgium.	Belgium.
Sweden.	Sweden.	Sweden.	Sweden.
Spain.	Spain.	Canada.	Canada.
Italy.	Canada.	Spain.	Spain.
—	Japan.	Italy.	Japan.
—	Italy.	Japan.	Italy.

CHAPTER V

THE MANUFACTURE OF FINISHED IRON

THE output of manufactured iron in Great Britain was at one time—only about twenty-five years ago—well on to three million tons a year. At that time the principal centres of the trade in finished materials were South Staffordshire, the north-east coast of England, and South Wales, each of which produced from 750,000 tons to about a million tons of puddled iron annually. The total output of such iron in each of the years 1902 and 1903 has been under a million tons, of which the largest quantity is still produced in South Staffordshire, and the next largest in Scotland, while the third and fourth places are taken by the Cleveland district and Lancashire, respectively.

The principal finished iron products of the present time are bar iron, sheets, rounds and squares, hoops, and wire rods. Bar iron represented about 40 per cent. of the total make of finished iron in 1904.

The number of puddling furnaces available for use in Great Britain in 1880 was over 7,000. In 1904 this total had been reduced to 1,470, of which 304 were not in use. For the last twenty years there has been a gradual disappearance of works and plants that formerly carried on the finished iron industry, more especially in South Staffordshire and South Wales. In the former district a considerable number of the old works now roll steel blooms and billets, purchased in the open market, into sheets, hoops, and other finished products; while in South Wales it may be said that the finished iron industry, which made the reputation and the fortunes of the Guests and Crawshays, has been entirely wiped out.

The greatest British output of manufactured iron in one year was two and three-quarter million tons. This output was reached in the year 1882, which was the halcyon period of the finished iron trade. Immediately afterwards trade began to decline, and the process of decay has been ruthlessly followed up to the present time. The following figures compare the year 1882 with the year 1902 :—

WORLD'S OUTPUT OF MANUFACTURED IRON

	1882. Tons.	1902. Tons.
Great Britain . .	2,841,000	... 965,000
United States . .	2,494,000	... 1,920,000 [1]
Germany . .	1,496,000	... 820,000
France . .	1,073,000	... 639,000
Belgium . .	503,000	... 378,000
Sweden . .	275,000	... 200,000 [1]
Russia . .	298,000	... 328,000
Other countries . .	500,000	... 430,000 [1]
Totals . .	9,680,000	... 1,580,000

While the output of finished iron has declined, as shown by these figures, the production of steel has concurrently increased, from less than seven millions to more than thirty-six millions of tons. The field in which steel has mainly dispossessed finished iron has been that of railway material. This change had been almost entirely consummated before 1890. Between that year and 1900 the displacement of finished iron for shipbuilding purposes

[1] There are no separate returns of the output of finished iron in 1902, so that the amount has had to be mainly estimated.

was in vigorous progress, and to-day, of the total quantity of materials used in shipbuilding, probably more than 90 per cent. takes the form of steel—mainly of the open-hearth variety.

The following short table shows the situation and resources of the plants engaged in the production of finished iron in Great Britain in 1904:—

FINISHED IRON WORKS IN THE UNITED KINGDOM

Scotland	.	.	16 works	...	277	furnaces
S. and W. Yorkshire	16	,,	...	212	,,
Cleveland	.	.	10	,,	...	221	,,
Lancashire	.	.	12	,,	...	167	,,
South Staffordshire	.	40	,,	...	270	,,
Shropshire	.	.	4	,,	...	40	,,
North Staffordshire	.	4	,,	...	80	,,

In Germany the number of works still engaged in this industry in 1903 was 156 against 164 in 1901 and 174 in 1900. The number of workmen employed in 1903 was 27,479 against 31,565 in the previous year. Here, as in the case of pig iron, a larger output coincided with a greatly reduced number of hands, but this may be due as much to the greater regularity of manufacturing operations in 1903 as to their greater efficiency. Of the total production of finished iron in 1903, 662,723 tons took the form of merchant iron, and 44,854 tons—the next largest item—that of plates and sheets. Tubes also come close to this figure.

There are still ninety-two works in Russia engaged in this industry, but a number of them are quite small forges. In 1902 the total production of puddled bar was 419,786 tons, while that of finished products was 327,915 tons. This means that the average output of finished material per establishment was under 3,600 tons. Much the largest number of works is found in the Oural, and

E

especially in the regions of Peru, Oufa, and Orenbourg. Nine of these works, with an output in 1901 of 20,000 tons of finished material, belong to the Crown.

The United States, Austria-Hungary, Sweden, and some other countries, have failed of late years to publish separate statistics of this industry, because of the difficulty of separating the two materials, which results from the rapid and important changes made in the direction of displacement by steel.

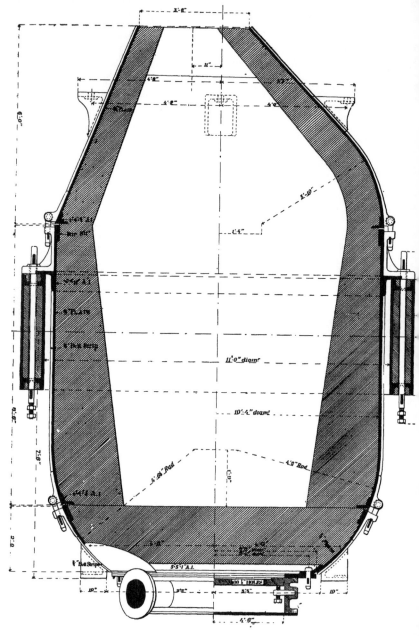

BESSEMER CONVERTER

CHAPTER VI

THE BESSEMER STEEL INDUSTRY.

I N the year 1879, when I wrote my work on *Steel: Its History, Manufacture, Properties, and Uses*, the discovery of the basic process of steel production had just been announced, the world's production of open-hearth steel did not exceed *two* million tons, the total output of Bessemer steel throughout the world was not much over *three* million tons, and for the first time, the United States came almost abreast of the British output, which it exceeded in the following year.

During the intervening period the growth of the steel manufacture, from every point of view, has presented the most remarkable phenomena to be found in the history of manufactures.

Originally, and until about thirty-five years ago, the British steel industry was carried on almost entirely in Sheffield and its neighbourhood. One or two establishments outside, such as the Newburn steelworks at Newcastle-on-Tyne, did, indeed, produce a certain quantity, but it was extremely limited. Until the year 1860 the quantity of steel yearly produced in Great Britain did not exceed 100,000 tons, and the output of the whole world was not twice that quantity annually. The steel then produced was almost wholly of the variety known as crucible, puddled, or cementation, and its cost was heavy, both because it was produced from expensive material—

Swedish bar iron—and because the process of manufacture
was long and costly. Up to about 1860 very little steel
was produced at a less cost than £20 per ton, and much
of the product went up to £50 and £60. Some twenty-
five years ago, the late Mr. Samuda, a well-known Thames
shipbuilder, furnished me with a statement of the steel
which he had used in ships built by his firm between 1858
and 1878.[1] At the earlier date ship plates cost £40 to
£50 per ton, and angles were £40. At the later date
plates cost £13 to £15, and were produced by the open-
hearth process. Less than twenty years afterwards plates
produced by the same process at the same works were sold
for £5 per ton.

The earlier works, designed and built to produce steel
by the Bessemer and open-hearth processes seem to have
been located in localities convenient to the sources of
supply of raw material, to the sources of demand, and to
ports of shipment. Scotland was chosen for a centre of
the steel industry about 1870, because the shipbuilding
industry was likely to make large demands upon steelworks. Wales was selected, both because steel was rapidly
superseding wrought iron as a material of construction,
and because the tin-plate and other industries carried on
in Glamorganshire and Monmouthshire promised to provide an increasingly important market. The Cleveland
district was chosen for the same reasons. These three
districts were, and remain, the most important steel-producing regions in Great Britain, measured by output.
Sheffield, however, has remained the greatest centre of the
trade in special wares, such as cutlery, hardware, munitions
of war, naval requirements of all kinds, small steel
castings, and a thousand and one other manufactures that
make up what is known as the Sheffield trades. The

[1] This statement will be found at pp. 716-17 of my work on *Steel: Its
History, Manufacture, and Uses.*

same city has retained almost from the first a virtual monopoly of the crucible steel industry, the products of which are still sold at very high prices for special purposes.

So far as the Bessemer process is concerned, it still holds the field, although not in Great Britain, where the output of open-hearth steel has now reached nearly twice the volume produced by Bessemer's system. A general impression has prevailed for years that the Bessemer will ultimately be displaced by the open-hearth process. The late A. L. Holley prophesied nearly thirty years ago that "the open-hearth process would attend the funeral of the Bessemer." This prophecy, like the foretold destruction of the malleable iron industry, which has been common over the last quarter of a century, is a long time of realising fulfilment. In the United States, Germany, Belgium, France, and, indeed, in almost all important steel-making countries except Great Britain, the Bessemer process still dominates. At the same time, there can be no doubt that the open-hearth is making relatively much greater progress.

The story of the origin and development of the Bessemer process since it was first announced in 1856 has been so often told that it would be but repeating a thrice-told tale to speak of it again. Perhaps the most remarkable feature of the story is that at the time he took up the subject of steel manufacture Sir Henry knew little or nothing of the metallurgy of iron. This he has described as being rather in his favour than otherwise, for he adds: "I find that persons wholly unconnected with any particular business are the men who make all the great inventions of the age." This is so far true that if we look over the history of the greatest inventions, we shall trace very few of a really revolutionary character that were due to the so-called practical man employed in the industries affected. Bessemer's experience and success are a curious and instructive commentary on the generally narrow-minded and often mistaken idea that practical men alone can accomplish any good thing.

When the pneumatic process was first submitted to the world, the iron manufacturers received it with coldness, not to say indifference and incredulity. Probably Sir Henry himself would say that the work of inventing was the easiest part of his task ; his serious difficulties lay in persuading those whom he desired to influence that there was anything in his system that was of value. This, indeed, proved so formidable a difficulty that he found it impossible to conquer it, except by the practical demonstration of what he could do in works of his own, which, accordingly, he proceeded to erect in Sheffield, in the very centre of the trade that he was intending to displace. Here he was able to afford the most convincing proof of the value of his process, the proof that he could make steel for not more than £10 per ton, which the crucible-steel manufacturers were selling at four or five times that amount, and as a consequence he was soon able to amass a large fortune as a manufacturer, not to speak of the royalty payments which he secured during the currency of his patents, and which he has himself declared to have amounted to considerably over a million sterling.

Having the whole ironmaking world more or less arrayed against him, Bessemer had to secure friends and co-workers by hook or by crook. He thereupon divided Great Britain into five principal ironmaking districts, and arranged to secure one ironmaster in each who would always work for him, by having a substantial interest in the success of his process. His plan was that each iron-master, by paying only one year's royalty on a quantity of Bessemer steel to be decided by himself, should pay no other royalty during the fourteen years of the patent. This proposal worked like a charm, and it deserves to be mentioned to the credit of the Dowlais Company that they were the first to take a licence under the scheme.

Even now, however, the troubles of the inventor were by no means at an end. The process worked with unfailing success up to a certain point; but the fact that it would only work the purest qualities of iron, and that the virtues of manganese were needed to make it complete, had still to be determined. The ironmasters of the South Staffordshire district, six weeks after Sir Henry's paper on his process was read at Cheltenham in 1856, met in solemn conclave, and decided that the process was a failure. The ground had therefore to be gone over again ; the steps toilfully taken over many months of vexatious experiments and costly trials had to be retraced. Bessemer now began to make experiments with manganese, having learned of the virtues of that metal from his study of the metallurgical works of the day, and especially from the miserable story of the life of Josiah Marshall Heath, who had introduced it into the crucible-steel trade of Sheffield. Many experiments with metallic manganese had been made by Bessemer, and he had practically reached the goal of his efforts, when Robert Mushet took out a patent for the application of a mixture of powdered manganese with pitch, which was afterwards stamped to a powder, and this he proposed to blow in at the bottom of the converter through the tuyeres. A later patent of Mushet's was for a triple compound of carbon, iron, and manganese; and other patents followed which were intended to cover every possible mode of introducing that material into steel manufactured by Bessemer's process.

Mushet's patents were never, however, acknowledged by Bessemer, and that for many reasons. In his own specifications, which antedated Mushet's, Bessemer mentioned

the use of manganese and of other substances as essential
features of his process.   Heath's patent covered largely
the same ground, and a triple compound of carbon, iron,
and manganese had, as he found, been used for many
years in Prussia.   Not only so, but Sir Henry's experiments themselves had practically covered the ground before Mushet came into the field.   As the £50 stamp due
on Mushet's batch of manganese patents at the end of
three years was not paid, the patents became void, and
Mushet's claims on the Bessemer process, if he ever had
any, were extinguished.

The name of Mushet has been so prominently associated
with Bessemer's great inventions that a few facts as to his
career may here be interpolated.   He was the son of
David Mushet, who was known to fame as the discoverer
of the famous blackband of Scotland, as the author of the
well-known work entitled *Papers on Iron and Steel*, and
as being one of the first to apply scientific research to the
ordinary operations of the blast furnace and the forge.
Robert Mushet had, therefore, an exceptional training as a
metallurgist for that time of day, and one of his fixed
aims was to cheapen and improve the quality of steel, of
which for many years he was a manufacturer.   Constant
ill-health during the last thirty years of his life affected
his prospects and his temper, but he was, nevertheless,
a frequent writer on metallurgical subjects, and what he
wrote was generally well worth attention.

A commonly received opinion of Bessemer steel has
been that it is a material of great toughness, containing
a small percentage of carbon and being " only one remove
from iron."   Striking illustrations of its ductility were
shown at an early stage, as, for instance, a round bar, two
inches in diameter, tied while cold in a knot with no break
of the fibre.   A well-known English house sent to the
Russian Exhibition many years ago a Bessemer railway

axle tied in a knot. That axle was afterwards presented to the United States Government, and is now to be seen in the National Museum at Washington. Bessemer steel was, at the outset, thought to be quite unfitted for very many uses for which cast crucible steel was formerly exclusively employed, especially the making of cutting instruments. But it was afterwards much modified and improved in its manufacture. It is certainly now much more than "one remove from iron," and it is employed for a great number of purposes for which crucible steel was formerly thought to be indispensable. On account of its greater cheapness, the sharp competition in trade, and the modifications which adapt it to a greater variety of uses, Bessemer steel, Siemens-Martin, and basic steel have largely been superseding crucible steel and crowding it out of the market. This, of course, cannot be done entirely, yet it is admitted by our best steelmakers that it is nearly impossible for the most experienced to decide by the fracture whether a given sample of steel is Bessemer or crucible. It is also an open secret that thousands of tons of Bessemer steel are sold annually as "cast" steel for the home as well as foreign markets. One of Sheffield's best makers says he has charged his manager to be careful to label all his steel, so as to distinguish between Bessemer cast steel and crucible cast steel.

Until 1886 Great Britain was the most important producer among the steel-manufacturing nations. In that year, however, our steel production was exceeded by that of the United States. Fifteen years later we were similarly eclipsed by Germany. Of the present-day steel output of the three countries, amounting to a total of about 28,000,000 tons, about 58 per cent. is produced by the United States, about 27 per cent. is produced by Germany, and about 15 per cent. is produced in Great Britain.

CHAPTER VII

THE OPEN-HEARTH STEEL INDUSTRY

THE history of the Siemens, Siemens-Martin, or open-hearth process, as it is variously described, is a short one. It only came into existence on a really practical scale about 1870, although more or less experimental works had been carried on by its distinguished inventors some years previous to that date. To-day, more than fifteen million tons of steel are annually produced by this process, of which three and a half millions are produced in Great Britain. The largest producer, however, is the United States, which, having early espoused the Bessemer process, and carried it to a notable stage of progress, did not enter the field with the open-hearth until a comparatively recent date. The recent advances of the open-hearth process have been much greater than those made by the rival process that bears the name of Bessemer.

Beyond all comparison, the most important event in the history of the steel industry next to the discovery and application of the Bessemer process in the period 1855–60 has been the application by the late Sir William Siemens of the regenerative furnace to the production of steel by the fusion of pig metal and scrap upon the open-hearth, or what is commonly known as the Siemens-Martin process, of which several modifications have since been adopted. This process is now usually spoken of as the open-hearth process. Its progress has been very rapid

58

OPEN-HEARTH STEEL-MELTING PLANT AT RIVER DON WORKS, SHEFFIELD

during recent years. In Great Britain the annual output of open-hearth steel now exceeds three million tons. In other countries the total output is about twelve million tons annually, so that the aggregate of the world exceeds fifteen million tons per annum, as already stated.

Perhaps the most distinguishing difference between the Bessemer and the open-hearth processes is that the former takes about fifteen minutes, and the latter takes six to eight hours to consummate. This difference of time enables the open-hearth product to be more carefully tested and examined while the process of manufacture is in progress; and hence it has been claimed that the open-hearth product can not only be made more varied in its characteristics—soft or hard within important limits— but is altogether more uniform. At an early stage the product of the Bessemer converter was more than suspected of brittleness and treachery. It has now out- lived this period of youthful indiscretions, but it is still distrusted for many important uses, and, indeed, for most purposes calling for a reliable and uniform material, open- hearth steel is prescribed. Bessemer steel manufacturers, nevertheless, maintain that no product can be more reliable than carefully-made Bessemer steel, and there are works engaged in that industry with so high a reputation as fully to confirm this claim.

Vast strides have been of late years attained in the technical and economic aspects of the open-hearth steel business. The earlier furnaces built, and some still em- ployed, had and have a capacity of only two and a half to five tons. To-day very few such furnaces are built with a smaller capacity than twenty-five tons, and fifty-five-ton furnaces are not at all uncommon. In general use, however, thirty-five-ton to forty-ton furnaces are perhaps the most ordinary practice. The recent improvements in this process, introduced by Talbot and Bertrand-Thiel, point to the ultimate adoption of double furnaces, capable of producing 200 tons to 300 tons, and justify the expectation that a much smaller number of plants will achieve the production now called for at a considerable economy of cost.[1]

The productiveness of open-hearth plants has greatly increased during recent years. Only about twenty years ago the average annual output of the individual furnace did not in Great Britain exceed 5,000 tons. To-day in the best open-hearth practice the average has risen to 20,000 tons, or four times as much. This great advance is not alone due to the increase in size of the furnace employed, but also to the mechanical improvements introduced in other directions, of which the charging machines introduced by Wellman and the electric cranes introduced by Morgan are not the least important.

The number of works engaged in the production of open-hearth steel in Great Britain has of late years greatly increased. There are now 95 works in operation in this country, which have collectively more than 520 open-hearth furnaces in operation. At a low estimate these furnaces are equal to the production of 4,500,000 tons of open-hearth steel annually.

The open-hearth process, whereby nearly $3\frac{1}{2}$ million tons of steel are now annually made in Great Britain, was projected by the late Sir William Siemens about 1863. An important stage of the progress of this system was the invention of the regenerative furnace, which, founded on the researches of Sir William Siemens into the theory of heat, was, nevertheless, primarily the idea of his brother Frederick, who conceived the view that the regenerative principle, which William, for a number of years, had been

---

[1] Talbot furnaces have been installed at the Cargo Fleet, Dowlais, and Frodingham Works, while Bertrand-Thiel furnaces are either projected or being proceeded with at the Round Oak Works of Lord Dudley, and at the Brymbo Works in South Wales.

trying to carry into effect, by a complex arrangement of engines and condensers, might be made available in a much more simple manner by its direct application to ordinary fuel-consuming furnaces. The invention founded on this idea was first brought before the world in a paper read by Sir William Siemens before the Institution of Mechanical Engineers in 1857, and one of the first practical applications was that made by the late E. A. Cowper in 1857 to the heating of the air for the stoves attached to iron-smelting furnaces.

Not long afterwards William Siemens applied the re-generative furnace to the puddling of iron, and at a later stage again it was made the basis for his well-known open-hearth process for the manufacture of steel — a process whereby we have seen that two-thirds of the total British make of steel is now produced, and one which has been of the greatest possible value to the commerce and industry of the world in cheapening the cost of ship construction and transport. Of the relative proportions of credit that are due to the brothers Siemens, and of the extent to which the success of the open-hearth furnace was facilitated by the co-operation of M. Emile Martin, of Sireuil, we need not speak here. Suffice it to say that their joint exertions and inventions have been the founda-tion of one of the largest and most essential industries of modern times.

The two rival processes of steel manufacture have, almost naturally, and in accordance both with their own characteristics and aptitudes, and with the requirements of trade, settled down into the cultivation of distinct spheres. The Bessemer process holds the field for railway material, structural material in the form of girders, pillars, blooms and billets, etc., for everyday use, while the open-hearth process has been preferred for shipbuilding purposes, for sheets, hoops, and other forms and purposes that call for special ductility and softness, as well as for a material that is uniform, regular, and reliable.

The steel-rail industry was originally located at Barrow, at Sheffield, and in South Wales. At a later date, West Cumberland and Cleveland came into the field. The total number of steel-rail manufacturing establishments in the country in 1903 was eight, and the output of steel rails was about 800,000 tons.

Ship plates and angles are chiefly produced in Scotland and on the north-east coast. The total average annual output of both, over the period 1888–1903, was about a million and a half tons. The largest individual producer is the Consett Company in Durham, which has an output of over 300,000 tons a year. The total number of works producing steel plates and angles is about ten, but the number varies from year to year.

The third most important branch of the steel trade is the manufacture of tin-plate bars, of which probably half a million tons are annually called for by the tin-plate works of Great Britain. This industry is chiefly carried on in South Wales, and of recent years a number of the established tin-plate works in that centre have built steel-works in order to guarantee their own supplies. In very few cases, however, are such steelworks carried on in connection with blast furnaces, so that not only do they require to buy their raw material, but they lose the advantage of the initial heat so secured. (See Appendix A.)

The sheet industry is one of great importance apart from tin plates. This industry is carried on largely in South Wales, where the largest works—those of J. Lysaght & Co.—have a total annual capacity of some 200,000 tons. The next most important works—those of Summers & Co. —are carried on near Chester, on the estuary of the Dee. Numerous sheet works exist in South Staffordshire and in the tin-plate manufacturing districts of the Principality, plants having of late years been erected to enable tin-plate workers to fall back on sheets when their regular trade was dull.

The manufacture of steel castings is now carried on in this country to a considerable and an increasing extent. The principal centre of this industry is the Sheffield district, where more than a dozen firms are engaged in it, some of them on a very large scale. The largest individual concern engaged in this business is the Hadfield Steel Foundry Company, which has the greatest steel foundry in Great Britain, if not in Europe, and whose principal products are projectiles and other war materials, wheels, axles, colliery tubs, and, indeed, almost every variety of work to which castings can be applied. Steel castings are now superseding steel forgings, if, indeed, they have not already wholly done so for most purposes. Nearly every enterprise engaged in producing steel forgings has now made provision for the manufacture of castings, and built-up crank-shafts and similar structures are becoming more or less things of the past. There is, however, no record of the extent to which this industry is carried on. The British output of steel castings in all categories must now be very considerable, and I should not place it at less than 130,000 tons. A steel foundry has become a recognised adjunct of important engineering works, and such foundries are carried on by great electrical firms, such as the Westinghouse Company, and by leading locomotive builders, such as Beyer, Peacock, & Co., as well as by firms that make the output of castings their main business, instead of a merely incidental and occasional operation.

Steel for Shipbuilding.—A considerable impetus was given to the development, both of the manufacture and the use of steel, by a paper read before the Institute of Naval Architects in 1875, by Sir Nathaniel Barnaby. In that paper, which I arranged with Sir Nathaniel to pre-

pare and read, the author made the following important
remarks :—

" The question we have to put to the steelmakers is,
what are our prospects of obtaining a material which we
can use without much delicate manipulation, and so much
fear and trembling? We have gone on for years using
iron plates, which are a compound of impure irons, of
different and unknown qualities, welded together imperfectly in the rolls. We want a perfectly coherent and
definitely carburised bloom, or ingot, of which the rolls
have only to alter the form in order to make plates with
qualities as regular and precise as those with copper or
gun-metal, and we look to the manufacturers for it. I am
ready, for my part, to go further than the French architects
have gone, and build the entire vessel, bottom plates and
all, of steel ; but I know that at present the undertaking
will involve an immense amount of anxiety and care.
We ought not to be behind any other country in this
matter."

While my friend Mr. James Riley was in charge of the
works at Landore, a series of experiments, extending
over some months, had been conducted, with a view to the
manufacture of plates, angles, etc., suitable for shipbuilding
and boiler-making, and as the results thereby got were
satisfactory, Mr. Gordon, the managing director at Landore, and Mr. Riley, as general manager, waited upon
Mr. Barnaby, informed him of what had been done at
Landore, and accepted the challenge he had laid down to
supply the material that would answer all the requirements
indicated. The result was that in the same year a contract
was entered into between the Admiralty and the Landore
Company for the supply by the latter of the plates, angles,
and beams to be used in the construction of the two
armed despatch vessels, the *Iris* and the *Mercury*.

For the purpose of this contract, and for the satisfaction

of the Admiralty generally, an elaborate series of tests was carried out on open-hearth steel made at Landore works, the results of which were stated in the valuable paper read by Mr. Riley before the Institute of Naval Architects in 1876. This may be regarded as the first serious start in applying steel to shipbuilding. Steel had hardly been applied at all to mercantile shipbuilding until the year 1876, when eleven vessels were constructed. In 1879 the new era was opening in full force, and Mr. Nathaniel Barnaby, in a paper which he read before the Iron and Steel Institute, intimated that the modified attitude towards steel of the various departments chiefly concerned in its use "was a veritable beginning of a great and inevitable change." At that very time nine ships were being built of steel at the works of Denny Brothers, Dumbarton, and two others were under construction by Messrs. R. Napier and Co. But even then the shipbuilders appeared to be dubious about using it. Dr. Kirk stated in 1879 that "steel had cracked in a mysterious manner," and he gave examples of failure that did not tend to assist its further use. As in the last five years more than 1,400,000 tons of open-hearth steel have been manufactured annually in this country for ship-building purposes alone, iron and timber ships have largely become things of the past.

F

CHAPTER VIII

THE BASIC AND CRUCIBLE
STEEL-MANUFACTURING PROCESSES

BASIC STEEL

TWENTY-THREE years after the Bessemer steel process had become one of the recognised methods of steel production, and sixteen years after the open-hearth process had been announced to the world by Siemens, the steel-manufacturing community was startled by the announcement of the discovery of a method of eliminating phosphorus from impure ores, and so enabling those ores to be for the first time applied to the production of commercial steel. The first intimation of this discovery was made at a meeting of the Iron and Steel Institute, in May, 1878, by Sidney G. Thomas, who, however, on that occasion limited himself to the declaration that he had succeeded in reducing the then objectionable metalloid named to a mere trace in the Bessemer converter. This had been the aim of metallurgists for many years, and it had absorbed much of the time, experience, and efforts of such notable metallurgical authorities as Lowthian Bell, Bessemer, Krupp, and Siemens, but without practical success. Thomas was then entirely unknown, so that his statement did not attract much attention, nor inspire much hope. On the contrary, I can well remember that it was received with a smile of incredulity that was not entirely without a certain amount of justification, in view of previous failures by others.

Some months later I received from the same gentleman

a visit at the offices of the Iron and Steel Institute, in the course of which he repeated his claim, and gave me some particulars of his experiments and their results. I at once saw that the matter was of the first importance, involving as it did the possibility of applying two-thirds of the ores of this country, then excluded from use in the manufacture of steel by the injurious effect of phosphorus, to that purpose, and I suggested that he should prepare a paper to be read before the Iron and Steel Institute meeting at Paris, in the autumn of 1878. Thomas undertook to do so, and the paper was duly presented to the Institute. There was, however, no time to have it read and discussed at Paris, and hence it was held over till the next meeting of the Institute in London, in May, 1879. This was a great occasion. Leading iron and steel manufacturers from every ironmaking country attended the meeting. The occasion was of more importance to Germany and France than to Great Britain, because the store of phosphoric iron ores possessed by those countries was relatively greater than that owned by Great Britain, and, indeed, none had any indigenous supplies of ore suited to the then requirements of the steel industry worth speaking of. Thomas, therefore, got much greater encouragement than either Bessemer or Siemens had done in the earlier stages of their great inventions. The basic process, as it was afterwards called, came at the true psychological moment. Great Britain, France, and Germany were the only important steel-producing nations of Europe. The boundaries of that industry were fixed by the available supplies of suitable non-phosphoric ores. Great Britain then produced over two million tons of such ores in West Cumberland, but from indigenous resources she could not have produced much over a million tons of steel annually. In France and Germany the similar possibilities were even more limited, and the only ores of importance then available were imported from Spain, Elba, Algeria, or other countries. Relying on such ores, it is probable that the output of steel in Europe could not at any time have easily been carried beyond ten million tons. The output of European steel to-day is at the rate of eighteen million tons, of which fully nine million tons are produced by the process introduced by Sidney G. Thomas under the conditions just related. Of this output over seven million tons are produced in Germany, and one million each in France and Great Britain. The output of basic steel in the United States was not taken up until within the last seven years, but the production to-day is at the annual rate of over five million tons, and it is clear that there, also, the steel industry could not have expanded as it has done but for the basic process.

There is much uncertainty as to the future of the steel industry of the world in relation to not a few problems of a more or less fundamental character, but there appears to be comparatively little doubt that there will be increased reliance on phosphoric ores, and that consequently the output of basic steel will relatively become much greater than it now is. Germany has vast stores of such ores, but hardly any other. We have seen that Great Britain has, in Cleveland, Lincolnshire, and the Midlands, enormous unutilised supplies of phosphoric ores, while the non-phosphoric varieties are mined only in Cumberland and North-west Lancashire in yearly diminishing quantities, and the production of this description is now only about 12 per cent. of the whole British output. Belgium relies almost entirely on the phosphoric ores of Luxembourg, Alsace, and the Moselle. France produces four-fifths of her total indigenous ore supplies in the phosphoric region of the Meurthe-et-Moselle. Even Sweden, distinguished in metallurgical annals as the home of the purest iron-making materials, is now supplying other nations with

phosphoric ores on a large scale. Canada has a good deal
more phosphoric ores than any other variety. The same
remark applies to Austria-Hungary, apart from the exceptionally high-class ores of the Styrian Erzberg.
Finally, in the United States, the largest and most important of all ascertained ore deposits, and the ore that is
to-day most largely worked, supplies mainly phosphoric
material. On the other hand, the available supplies of
non-phosphoric ores, hitherto limited mainly to the Marquette, Vermilion, and Gogebic ore ranges of Lake
Superior, in the United States, to the Bilbao region in the
North of Spain, and to one or two less important regions
elsewhere, are yearly decreasing in volume, and in some
cases have come very near to exhaustion. In Great
Britain the output of such ores over the last few years has
not much exceeded one-half of that of twenty years ago.
Clearly, therefore, in the light of present knowledge and
experience the basic process must mainly respond to the
increased demands of the future.

The most notable, and in some respects the most admirable, feature of the basic process is that it can be, and
generally is, carried on with the same equipment and plant
as those employed for the ordinary so-called acid, or non-
phosphoric steel-manufacturing system of Bessemer and
Siemens. The rationale of the process differs mainly in the
lining used for the vessel or hearth employed, and in the
treatment of the steel under conversion. The lining has
to be made of material carrying more or less considerable
quantities of limestone, which absorbs the phosphorus.
Additions of lime are applied during the blow, if in
the Bessemer converter, and during the heat, if in the
open-hearth furnaces, in order to complete this absorption.
These two features necessarily call for a certain additional
outlay on the basic process, but that is compensated for by
the lower cost of the iron employed, which is usually 5*s*. to

10s. per ton under the concurrent cost of hematite or Bessemer iron. Against this, also, there is the cost of basic slag, which, containing as it does a high percentage of phosphorus, is of considerable value for fertilising purposes.

CRUCIBLE STEEL

Reference has already been made to the early history of this branch of the steel industry, which, until the advent of Bessemer, was practically the only one carried on to any material extent. The industry was founded on the importation into Great Britain of Swedish bars of a very pure description. These bars were made from Dannemora ore, and have sold in England as high as £36 per ton,[1] although in later years they fell as low as £10 to £12 per ton. It is unnecessary to enter into details of the process or of the equipment employed. The distinguishing methods applied in producing shear, blister, cementation, puddled, and so-called natural steel, and such various equipment as the Catalan forge, the Wülf's oven, the blomary fire, the blue oven, the ordinary pot-steel melting hole, and kindred details, are all to be found set out in a previous work by the writer,[2] and in most of the complete metallurgical treatises.

The greatest quantity of crucible steel produced in this country in any one year was probably well under 100,000 tons. I do not believe that that figure has ever been exceeded, but it is difficult to speak with confidence on the subject, as the statistics of the trade have not been systematically collected at any period in its history. Sanderson[3] computed the total output of crucible steel in 1848 at 40,000 tons. In the same year the volume of

[1] This price was the one that ruled in 1854.
[2] *Steel: Its History, Manufacture, and Uses*, by J. S. JEANS.
[3] *Journal of the Society of Arts*, 1854.

crucible steel produced in France was about 15,000 tons; in Austria 13,000 tons; and in the United States about 10,000 tons. Up to the same period, the greatest quantity of Swedish bar iron imported into Great Britain in any one year was 35,500 tons in 1851.

The natural tendency of all more expensive processes is to be displaced by less costly methods. The crucible-steel industry, which was almost the only one of any real importance forty years ago, has been gradually superseded by one or other of the newer systems of Siemens and Bessemer. Material that cost £25 to £80 per ton is not likely to continue to hold its own on equal terms with material that can be sold at £5 to £10 per ton. This is the present situation in the steel industry.

The manufacture of the steel available prior to the Bessemer process was both tedious and expensive. The general cost of conversion has been stated by a highly experienced manufacturer at 26s. per ton, and the average cost of melting is computed at £8 5s. per ton, of which 6s. in the former case, and 50s. in the latter, are assigned to wages alone, while 10s. and 75s. or 85s. in all, are assigned to coal and coke. As these figures do not include the cost of the iron used, nor that of forging, which may be taken at anything between £30 and £35 per ton, according to the period and the conditions, it need hardly be added that crucible steel was and is necessarily a costly product, and when it is added that from start to finish the process occupied several weeks, and could only be applied to more or less homœopathic quantities, the limited character of the industry may be easily understood.

One of the distinguishing characteristics of the crucible-steel industry is the wide range of tempers aimed at and produced, classified according to the percentage of carbon, which runs from ¾ to 1½ per cent.

The crucible-steel manufacturer has to produce at least

eight different qualities of final product from as many
different grades of material, each costing a different price.
Each of these qualities may be made of seven different
tempers, which gives fifty-six different kinds of steel,
varying in the percentages of metalloid, in temper, and in
other conditions. Not only so, but each of these different
grades of steel may be, and more or less is, produced by
four different methods. The crucible-steel industry embraces a large number of so-called special steels, varying
according to the percentage of carbon, tungsten, wolfram,
manganese, or other alloying material employed. These
special steels have in previous periods been sold in
Sheffield up to £130 per ton, and for a number of years
Huntsman's regular price was £76.[1]

Of late years, the crucible-steel manufacturers of Sheffield
have employed considerable quantities of both Bessemer
and open-hearth steel, used ostensibly with extraordinary
care, but in some cases with much less care than in others,
to displace Swedish bar iron as the raw material of the
crucible industry. The process of manufacture remains
substantially the same, which means that while Bessemer
and open-hearth steel can be produced in blooms or billets
at little more than £3 10s. per ton, a billet of crucible
steel, disregarding the cost of Swedish bars or common
steel scrap employed, would cost £15 to £16 for manipulation alone—conversion, melting, and forging.

It is not a matter for surprise under these circumstances
that the crucible-steel industry has not succeeded in holding its own. Even in Sheffield open-hearth steel is now
extensively applied to many purposes formerly filled by
the products of the crucible; but for the highest forms
of cutlery, tools, and instruments, crucible steel continues
to be used by firms of high standing and integrity.

[1] Paper read by Henry Seebohm in Sheffield, April, 1869.

CHAPTER IX

FOREIGN IRONMAKING COUNTRIES

THE UNITED STATES

IT is impossible to do more than give a perfunctory and imperfect summary of the vast ironmaking resources and magnificent development of the United States. The subject has been referred to elsewhere in the present volume in relation to various cardinal and controlling aspects of the trade; but a few additional particulars seem to be called for here.

It would be little short of ridiculous, however, to attempt to give even the outlines of the history of the development of the American iron industry. Every branch of that great organisation has a record of engrossing interest, whether regarded as a series of struggles against what seemed to be unfavourable conditions, or as a consequent series of triumphs over mechanical and financial difficulties, geographical and topographical conditions that were not suited to the requirements of the time, the imperfect organisation and education of labour, and isolation from the great markets of the world at a period when it took fifty to sixty days to cross the Atlantic.

In the year 1854 the total production of pig iron throughout the world was about 6,000,000 tons.[1] Of that quantity 3,000,000 tons were produced in Great Britain and only 750,000 tons in the United States, which latter

[1] According to Mr. J. K. Blackwell, in a paper read before the Society of Arts in London.

country consequently produced only 12½ per cent. of the whole. In the period 1871–85, the average annual production of pig iron by the United States had risen to 18·7 per cent. of that of the world generally. In the period 1886–96 the proportion had increased to 30·9 per cent., and during the last three years the United States have provided about 46 per cent. of the world's total supply.

This remarkable progress has been due to a variety of circumstances, some natural, some adventitious, of which the most commanding have been the vast coal and iron-ore resources of the Republic, the exceptional resourcefulness of the Americans in invention and in the capacity to excel, the accommodating character of American labour, and last, but not least, the encouragement given to industrial enterprise by the Customs tariff. The exceptionally great distances which Nature has interposed between the ore of Lake Superior and the coal of Pennsylvania have been overcome by methods of transportation that have set an example to the rest of the world, and have eclipsed all previous records in economy. The organisation of industry in iron-ore mines and cokeries, at blast furnaces, and in steelworks, has been carried out on a scale of magnitude never before approached. In the mechanical handling of materials, results have been achieved which for many years were regarded with incredulity by the slower-moving people of Europe. Finally, America has become more or less the academy to which all other iron-making nations have resorted for both precept and example not to be elsewhere secured.

For the first hundred years of its career, however, the American iron trade moved but slowly. That was a natural result of a sparse and limited population, a vast domain, much of which was a wilderness, attempts at repression and discouragement by the mother country, an imperfect acquaintance with the technique of the iron-

making arts, and a firmly grounded belief that agriculture
alone was to maintain the country in a condition of high
prosperity. From this unfavourable situation the railway
and the steamship gradually relieved the trade. The railway demands that began to assume considerable proportions between 1860 and 1875, led to a notable increase
of enterprise. In the period 1871–85 the total quantity
of pig iron made in the United States was 46,000,000 tons,
and in the next ten years the output had grown to 86·4
million tons ; but the upward movement culminated with
an output of over 18,000,000 tons in 1903 alone.

The principal factor in enabling this progress to be
achieved was the discovery and development of the iron
ores of the Lake Superior ranges and of the coking coal of
the Connellsville region in Western Pennsylvania. Not,
however, that these were the only sources of supply.
Indeed, the returns for 1902 show that in that year hard
ores were mined in seventeen, and soft ones in twenty-
two, states and territories. But four-fifths of the total is
now produced on Lake Superior from 133 mines, of which
forty-eight on the Mesabi Range contribute well on to one-
half. The resources of this region have been computed as
equal to the maintenance of the present rate of consumption for more than sixty years.

The coke supplies of the United States are mainly
obtained from the Connellsville district, about an average
of fifty miles from Pittsburg. The coke is produced at
considerably less than any similar product in Europe,
and the freight to the blast furnaces in or around Pittsburg is about 4s. a ton. In some years a large part of
this coke was sold at about a dollar a ton at the ovens,
when similar coke in South Durham was costing 8s. to
12s. at ovens. The average price is, however, nearer 7s.
per ton at the ovens in West Pennsylvania. The coke
supply there is ample for many years to come.

As late as 1810 there were produced in the whole country only 917 tons of steel, Pennsylvania's share being 531 tons, or more than half of the whole. It is remarkable that the Keystone State still makes about the same relative percentage. Even in 1831 the production of steel was only 1,600 tons, an amount which was said then to equal the whole quantity imported, so that the market for steel was divided equally with the foreigner seventy years ago. But this steel was made chiefly by cementation; crucible steel was to come later. From 1831 until as late as 1860 very little progress was made in developing the manufacture of steel. The total product in 1850 was only 6,000 tons. In 1840 Isaac Jones and William Coleman began its manufacture in Pittsburg, and succeeded. Singer, Nimick, & Co., in 1853, produced successfully the usual grades of cast steel for saws, machinery, etc., and for kindred purposes. Hussey, Wells, & Co., in 1850, made the first crucible steel of first quality as a regular product obtained from American iron, and in 1862 came Park Brothers & Co., with the biggest steel plant of all up to that time. Several hundred English workmen were imported by this firm to ensure success. All these concerns were in Pittsburg.

In 1873 the United States produced 198,796 tons of steel; Great Britain, their chief competitor, 653,500 tons, more than three times as much. Twenty-six years later, 1899, the United States production was more than double that of Great Britain, the figures being 10,639,957 and 5,000,000 tons respectively, an eight-fold increase for Britain and fifty-three-fold for the United States.

The present centre of U.S. steel is the square made by a line drawn from Pittsburg to Wheeling, northward to Lorain, eastward to Cleveland, and south again to Pittsburg. In this territory most of the steel is made. Allegheny County alone (Pittsburg) in 1899 produced nearly one-quarter of all the pig iron in the United States, almost half of the open-hearth steel, and about 39 per cent. of the total production of all kinds of steel. As late as the middle of the last century the Eastern States upon the Atlantic constituted the home of steel manufacture. Even in Pennsylvania one-half of all the steel was made east of the Alleghany Mountains. Since then the trend has been constant and rapid to the region known as the Central West, which has Pittsburg as its metropolis.

The remarkable changes that have been accomplished in the pig-iron-making conditions of the United States have been put by Mr. C. Kirchhoff, of New York, in his Presidential Address to the American Institute of Mining Engineers in a statistical form which brings them readily home. These figures are summarised in the following short table, taking the year 1889 as 100, all expressed in percentages of that figure:—

	1900.	1898.
Product per day .	94·1 ...	167·7
Ore cost	107·6 ...	79·0
Limestone cost .	87·6 ...	40·3
Coke cost	99·4 ...	64·1
Labour cost	112·8 ...	51·9
Total cost	104·3 ...	63·4
Average selling price	103·0 ...	61·2
Average profit .	95·1 ...	47·9

The comparative cost of steel ingots as between 1891 and 1898, fell as shown in the following figures, taking the year 1889 as 100, expressed in percentages of that figure:

	1891.	1898.
Pig iron .	63·5 ...	41·5
Scrap .	11·9 ...	6·2
Spiegel .	12·2 ...	7·8
Limestone	·24 ...	·20
Fuel .	1·5 ...	1·6
Labour .	5·6 ...	4·2
Supplies, taxes, etc.	3·0 ...	1·8

The main cause, apart from exceptional natural resources, of the vast progress achieved by the iron and
steel industries of the United States is the enormous
extent of the home market. The American consumption
of steel *per capita* has gone up from 20 lb. to 500 lb.
within less than half a century. The cheapening of the
product has stimulated the demand for steel to an extent
that would not have been deemed possible only a quarter
of a century ago. New sources of demand have opened
up in every direction, and with amazing rapidity. While
railway demands have naturally all along been the most
considerable in a country that has a total extent of railway lines fully equalling that of the whole of Europe,
the requirements of agriculture—fencing, implements, etc.
—and of every other interest, have called for continually
increasing supplies. Within five years the demand for
rolling stock alone has risen from almost a minus quantity
to nearly 800,000 tons a year. Within ten years the
demands of the tin-plate industry have advanced from less
than 5,000 tons to about 500,000 tons annually. Within
the same short interval building demands have more than
trebled, and there are now but few structures that do not
make use of steel skeletons.

The most prominent commercial features of the
American steel industry during the last fifteen years
may be thus specified :—

1. An enormous expansion of output in every direction,
culminating in the doubling or more of the production of
both pig iron and steel and the various products thereof.

2. A constant increase in the relative proportions of
pig iron and steel, leading to the proportion of crude
steel to the pig-iron product being advanced from 46 per
cent. in 1890 to about 80 per cent. at the present time.

3. An increase of 200 per cent. to 300 per cent. in the

BLOOMING MILL AT THE DIFFERDINGEN WORKS, GERMANY

amount of product obtained from a given plant within a given time, alike at blast furnaces and in steelworks.

4. A remarkable reduction in the cost of labour per unit of product all over the country.

5. An unprecedented reduction in the cost of producing both pig-iron and steel products, whereby both costs and selling prices in the United States were for the first time brought below those of Europe.

6. A long period of depression under the influence of which these results were made possible by the strictest economy and mechanical and economic advances all along the line. (This period lasted from 1891 to 1898.)

7. A succeeding period of inflation, during which trusts and syndicates were established in every branch of the trade, culminating in the United States Steel Corporation —a merger of most of the great iron and steel producing concerns in the country with its capital of £280,000,000 sterling and its 170,000 operatives.

8. A strong and strenuous rivalry between the Steel Corporation and independent firms, which is still in progress, and of which the end is yet far to seek.

9. A notable appreciation in the value and the costs of raw materials, which appears likely to be maintained, due to the realisation of the fact that while the demand for steel may be indefinitely extended, the available supplies of iron ore and coking coal are fixed quantities, incapable of replacement or substitution.

10. A keen and watchful rivalry on the part of the leading manufacturing interests to keep in the front of mechanical advances and up-to-date conditions all round, leading to the attainment of much more remarkable results than have been attained in any other country.

On some of the more recent characteristics of the American steel trade I shall have occasion to speak later on.

GERMANY

While the manufactures of both iron and steel had been carried on in Germany during the Middle Ages, from the end of the Crusades to the beginning of the Thirty Years' War, yet the industry on an important scale is very modern—so much so, indeed, that the output of iron ores has increased nearly five-fold within the last thirty years. Fifty years ago the empire of to-day did not produce half a million tons of pig iron annually, while in 1904 the output was nearly ten and a half million tons, or more than twenty times as much. The output of steel has made still more remarkable strides. In 1850 the total German output of steel was less than 12,000 tons, whereas in 1904 it was close on 8,500,000 tons, or 700 times as much.

This remarkable growth has been mainly accomplished during the last ten years, and it is still proceeding at a pace which guarantees the attainment of much greater dimensions in the near future.

Germany has more abundant and valuable sources of domestic iron ores than any other European (continental) country except Spain, and probably even Spain has not the same volume of ores as that known to exist in the provinces of Alsace and Lorraine. Germany has also a great abundance of good coal, especially in Westphalia. So far her natural resources are excellent. But the ore and the fuel are more than a hundred and fifty miles apart, and can only be connected by the payment of railway rates to the tune of about 7s. per ton of material carried in either direction. The small coal-field of the Saar is nearer to Alsace than Westphalia, but it does not provide such good coke, nor in sufficient quantity.

Germany has five principal iron-mining centres, severally

tabulated as Bonn, Breslau, Clausthal, Luxembourg, and Lorraine. Of these five, two alone—Luxembourg and Lorraine—produce 80 per cent. of the total iron-ore output of the country, which in 1903 was about twenty million tons, and is officially computed as of an average value of 3·6 marks per ton, the average value of the ores of the two principal districts being only about 2·5 marks (2s. 6d.) per ton at the place of production. In the district of Bonn, however, more than two million tons are still produced of a higher quality of ore; the average value is stated at 10s. 6d. to 13s. per ton ; and in the districts of Breslau and Clausthal the average value of the output—less than a million tons for both—is from 4s. 3d. to 6s. 3d. per ton. The average yearly output of iron ore per miner employed in Luxembourg and Alsace-Lorraine ranges from 440 to 460 tons a year.

Germany, like England, has of late years required to supplement her own iron-ore output by constantly increasing imports from other countries. In 1870 those imports amounted to only about 300,000 tons; in 1880 they were 607,000 tons ; in 1890 they were 1,522,000 tons ; in 1900 they were 4,107,000 tons ; and in 1904 they were more than 4,500,000 tons. These extensive imports were mainly received from France—the Meurthe-et-Moselle—Sweden, and Spain. As regards the two latter districts, Germany competes with England for supplies, and has, in several cases, competed by paying higher prices.

Germany also exports considerable quantities of iron ores. Up to the year 1898, indeed, her exports had, taking one year with another, largely exceeded her imports, but this was due to the demands of Belgium and France for the ores of Luxembourg and Lorraine. In 1897 the German ore exports exceeded 3,230,000 tons, and in one year since then the figure has been still larger.

The German iron and steel industries are, as a whole,

G

much younger than those of Great Britain, and, speaking generally, they are also, as might be expected, more up-to-date. While there have been comparatively few new steel-works laid down in Great Britain during the last ten years, quite a number of new plants have been installed in Germany, some of them of very considerable dimensions. The general average output of the leading works in the Fatherland is considerably in excess of the leading British works. There are seventeen different works in Germany that each produce over 200,000 tons of steel annually, while not more than three or four works in Great Britain exceed that figure. In the year 1902, 103 different steel-works in the empire produced 7,780,000 tons of steel, which is an average of over 75,000 tons per establishment. The average output of British works, similarly computed, was not, in the same year, more than 40,000 tons.

The total production of different descriptions of steel in Germany and Luxembourg was as under, in the year 1903:—

				Tons.
Bessemer basic	.	.	.	4,888,000
„ acid	.	.	.	342,000
Open-hearth basic	.	.	.	2,304,000
„ acid	.	.	.	130,000
Crucible steel	.	.	.	117,000
Total	.	.	.	7,781,000

This steel was produced almost wholly in Westphalia, excepting about 2,200,000 tons produced in Alsace and Luxembourg.

The recent course of the German iron industry has in many ways been very remarkable. The production of different descriptions of iron and steel during the last ten years has by far exceeded that of any previous period of equal duration. In this interval, the production of iron ore has increased from 11½ to about 20 million tons ; of pig iron from 4·6 to 10·1 million tons ; of castings from 1·0 to 1·5 million tons ; of finished steel from 1·6 to 6 million tons ; and of steel of all kinds, including ingots and blooms and billets for sale, from 2·2 to about 8½ million tons. The output of finished iron has, however, declined over the same period, and is not now more than one-half of what it was.

The foundry industry of Germany is one of great extent and importance. While there are 108 pig-iron works, 164 finished-iron works, and 200 steelworks in Germany, there are no fewer than 1,249 foundries, or 777 works more than the sum of all the other three put together. These 1,249 foundries produced in 1900 1,812,604 tons of castings, and in 1901 reduced this figure to 1,520,617 tons, while the number of hands employed, concurrently, fell from 95,548 to 85,715. There is no detailed record of the products of these works, but it may be stated, as regards pipes, that the output was 271,964 tons in 1900, and 254,758 tons in 1901.

Nothing in the history of the iron industry has been more remarkable than the recent expansion of the foreign trade of Germany. Between 1898 and 1903 the exports of German iron and steel had fully doubled. Between 1901 and 1903 the exports of semi-products, half-manufactured steel, in the form of blooms and billets, had more than trebled in quantity, the exports of rails had more than doubled, the exports of pig iron had almost trebled, and the exports of most other descriptions had increased. In 1903 the total iron and steel exports of the Fatherland, which up to 1900 had made comparatively slow progress, had come almost abreast of those of Great Britain. This progress was largely attributable to the cultivation of the manufacture and sale of half-finished

products, which in the years 1902 and 1903 were produced, for sale, to the extent of over two million tons
annually, or fully three times as much as the output of
the same products in Great Britain.

So far as natural resources are concerned, Germany is
perhaps more nearly on a level with Great Britain than
any other European country.   Her iron-ore resources are
greater, and her coal and coke resources are fully as good,
but she has not the same advantages in respect of the
proximity of raw materials to each other and to ports of
shipment.   On the other hand, she has the command of
cheaper rates of transport, both by land and sea, and her
labour is both less costly and more easily controlled.
There would seem to be nothing to hinder the German
Empire from continuing a career of large development
and great achievements as an ironmaking country.

FRANCE

Unlike Germany, Great Britain, and the United States,
France has been more concerned with retaining her own
home markets against all comers than in reaching forward
to capture foreign markets.   She has been richly endowed
with certain requisites for a great iron industry, especially
in the ores of the Meurthe and the Moselle, and those endowments would have been much more ample had not the
events of the war of 1870–1 transferred to Germany the
one thing needful for the magnificent iron industry that
has been built up in the Fatherland—almost inexhaustible
supplies of the cheaply won ores suited to the basic
process of manufacturing steel.   The total French production of the ores in this region in 1870 was 1,214,000
tons.   In the same year the total production of pig iron
in France was 1,178,000 tons.   The industry at the time

of the war had therefore not assumed any very considerable dimensions. After the war it took a long time to recover. Between 1870 and 1877 there was an increase of only about 300,000 tons in the total make of pig iron. Technically the industry was also in a very backward condition, as may be concluded from the single fact that the 266 furnaces in blast in 1870 produced an average of only 4,400 tons a year, or about as much as some up-to-date furnaces can now produce in a single week.

At that time, and indeed all through the recent history of the French iron industry, it was carried on over a very wide range of provinces, but the leading producer has for the last half-century been the Meurthe-et-Moselle, which is, like most of the other provinces in which the industry is carried on, so landlocked as to tend to shut out foreign trade, whether as imports or as exports. The imports of iron and steel into France have for the last half-century greatly exceeded the exports, and for the greater part of the period they have been fully four times as much. The only works that are within a comparatively short distance of shipping facilities are those of the Nord and the Pas-de-Calais. Creusot, the leading establishment of this kind in the country, is more than 250 miles from the sea. The Loire, which has the greatest number of important works producing highly finished and largely competitive products, is similarly situated. Against this disadvantage, however, the French ironworks, except those of the Meurthe-et-Moselle, are mostly situated in the neighbourhood of coal-fields, which produce generally inferior coal.

Half a century ago the output of steel in France was 3,500 to 4,000 tons annually. By 1860 the Bessemer system had been adopted, and some few years later the Siemens-Martin process, one important branch of which originated in France, came into operation. In 1875 the total output of steel of all kinds exceeded 257,000 tons.

In 1904 the total production of finished French steel of all kinds was 1,482,708 tons.

The French steelworks can hardly be said to seriously compete with Great Britain and Germany for the general iron and steel markets of the world, and we rarely hear of foreign orders for rails, ship plates, hoops, sheets, girders, or other everyday products, falling to their lot. On the other hand, they do compete successfully in certain more or less special lines, and especially in alloys and war material. Considerable exports of pig iron, and even of rails and girders, etc., have occasionally been made by the works in the Meurthe-et-Moselle, shipping at Antwerp or other foreign ports. Both iron and steel can be made cheaply in this region. It has been recently computed, and from the evidence put before the writer it is believed authoritatively, that basic pig iron can be made by the German works in Alsace for from 35s. to 40s. per ton, and the conditions of the French works in the Meurthe are not greatly dissimilar. This brings the cost of pig iron near to the best results that can be pointed to in Great Britain.

The total output of the French iron and steel plants in 1904 was as follows, in metrical tons :—

Pig Iron.	Finished Iron.	Steel Ingots.
2,999,000	554,000	2,080,000

The technical and economic conditions of the French iron trade have materially improved during recent years. As a result, France has been taking a more prominent place as an iron-exporting country. It is not unlikely that in the future she may qualify to become a still more successful competitor in outside markets. It was not until within the last ten years that she made much effort as an exporting country, and to-day she is still far behind both Germany and the United States.

BELGIUM

This little country has made a remarkable record in the recent history of the iron industry, having regard to its limited dimensions and to its poor resources in coal and iron ore.   Indeed, it may well be doubted whether, with the exceptions of Holland and Italy, any notable European country has such meagre natural resources.   The production of domestic iron ores has been declining for a number of years past, and now amounts to only about 166,000 tons a year (in 1902 166,480 tons), which is not much more than a twentieth part of the annual consumption.   The balance is imported from Luxembourg, Alsace, and elsewhere.   The coal, of which the output is only about 24,000,000 tons a year (23,877,470 tons in 1902), is of an inferior quality, and is expensive to work, so that the average selling price is rarely under 11 francs per ton. The average annual output for ten to eleven hours' work is therefore only about 170 tons per workman employed above and below ground, against about 300 tons in England, and close on 300 tons in the Westphalian coal-field. Coke, for the same reasons, is exceptionally dear, and the average selling price over the last few years has been close on 20 francs per ton (19·32 francs in 1902).

The pig-iron industry of Belgium is chiefly located in the province of Liége.   The principal establishment is the great works at Seraing of the Société Cockerill, founded by an Englishman more than half a century ago.   There are altogether eighteen works engaged in this branch of the trade, which in 1902 employed thirty-three blast furnaces, and had seven others idle.   The total production of pig iron was in the same year 1,069,050 tons, which was more than twice the output of a quarter of a century ago. About one-half of this quantity was basic iron, and about a quarter was forge, the remainder being Bessemer and foundry qualities.

Belgium has held its own in regard to the manufacture of finished iron longer than any other European country except Russia. The total production of finished iron has not materially declined here, while in most other European countries, and in the United States, it has fallen to less than one-half of its former maximum. But the quantity was never very considerable. In 1902 it was 480,840 tons of puddled bars, etc., and 381,630 tons of finished-iron products, of which 260,290 tons took the form of merchant products.

There were still in 1902 fifty-one works in Belgium engaged in this branch of the iron industry, of which twenty-five were in the province of Hainault, and eighteen in the province of Liége. These works employed a total of 12,907 hands, 792 puddling and other furnaces, and 174 rolling mills.

The steel industry of Belgium has made relatively great strides within the last few years. Although steel had been made in this country prior to the advent of the Bessemer process, the first commercial attempt to carry on the manufacture was initiated in 1864, when Bessemer steelworks were built at Seraing, and 296 tons were produced. Ten years later this output had advanced to 36,584 tons, and from that period the progress of the industry has been pretty steady. The output of ingots in 1902 was 769,040 tons, and the output of finished steel was 743,260 tons. In that year there were nineteen steelworks in the kingdom, of which nine were in Hainault, five in Liége, and five in other provinces. These works unitedly employed 8,333 workmen, 46 Bessemer converters, 19 open-hearth and 90 reheating furnaces, and 53 rolling mills. The principal products of the steelworks were rails (268,220 tons in 1902), girders (109,390 tons), and merchant steel and special profiles (137,700 tons).   The production of ingots, blooms, and billets for sale in the same year was 198,290 tons.

Belgium is one of our most indefatigable competitors in foreign and colonial markets, and exports a relatively larger proportion of her iron and steel production than any other country.   This is due rather to the extreme care and economy exercised in every operation and department, to the industry of the workers, and to the low wages paid, than to the natural endowments of the country.   The average price of basic pig iron in 1902 is officially returned at 51s. 6d., which is about 1s. 6d. above the average in the Cleveland (Yorkshire) district; the average price of Belgium billets for the same year was returned at 79s. per ton; and the average price of steel rails is returned at 96s. per ton—prices which do not appear to beat those current in Great Britain on the score of cheapness.

SWEDEN

Sweden is one of the oldest, and in many respects one of the most interesting, iron-producing countries in the world.   Ample iron-ore resources, much of them of the very highest character, have enabled the Swedes to achieve and to maintain a character for excellence as metallurgists that has never been successfully challenged.   But the country is destitute of coal of suitable composition for ironmaking, and until quite lately the ores worked have been rather expensive, so that the products of the furnaces, mills, and forges of Sweden have not usually competed on the ground of cheapness with those of other countries. Nor has Sweden ever emulated the newer ironmaking countries in respect of the volume of production.   The principal products are pig iron, bar iron, sheets and hoops, rounds, and squares, etc.   The maximum annual output of pig iron has been about 600,000 tons ; of Bessemer ingots, 115,000 tons; of open-hearth ingots, 210,000; of blooms and billets, 226,000 tons ; while bars have always been under 200,000 tons.

Sweden employed, in 1902, 2,179 workmen in coal mines, 10,496 in iron-ore mines, and 15,255 in iron and steel works. In the same year there were in existence 186 iron and steel works, of which 35 were worked by private owners, 121 by limited companies, and 30 by other organisations.

The total value of the iron and steel output of Sweden in 1902 was as follows in Swedish crowns (1 S. Cr. = 1s. 1d.).

Output of Iron-mines.	Iron and Steel.
14,368,806	136,775,350

The *net* revenues earned by the iron mines and iron and steel works in the same period were, in the same currency, as under, in crowns :—

Iron-mines.	Iron and Steel Works.
3,389,681	4,700,714

The absence of coal and coke makes it necessary, and expedient, to make use of charcoal as a fuel, and, as is usual in such cases, the annual output of a given plant is small. The 152 blast furnaces in operation in Sweden in 1893 produced an average of 2,983 tons during the year, but in 1902 136 furnaces produced an average of 3,957 tons, so that here also there is evidence of progress. The greatest progress of all appears in the development of the iron-ore resources of the country, the production of which has more than doubled since 1893, and now runs to about three million tons annually, the greater part of which is exported to Germany, England, Belgium, and France.

Apart from the development of its iron-ore supplies and the satisfaction of the need of other countries, Sweden is not likely in the future to play a relatively more important part in the iron industry. But it fills a useful and necessary place ; its ironmasters are capable, careful, and not without enterprise, and in the future, as in the past, the country is likely to continue to provide the rest of the world with materials of the very highest class.

NORWAY

While Sweden is, relatively to its population and general economic situation, one of the most important ironmaking countries in Europe, it is quite otherwise with the other half of the late dual kingdom.   Norway did once produce pig iron and also a certain quantity of wrought iron, but both branches are now virtually extinct.   And yet in the middle of the eighteenth century Norway had as many as seventeen ironworks, which produced and exported iron to most of the countries of Europe, including Great Britain.   The output, however, was never very large.   The available records show that in 1781 the output of pig iron and castings was 8,215 tons ; in 1806 6,320 tons ; and in 1895 348 tons.   Since the latter year the industry has ceased to exist.   The pig iron produced was of the charcoal variety, and one establishment—that carried on by Count Laurvig—had three blast furnaces and eleven refining furnaces at one time in operation.   The final extinction of the Norwegian iron industry is attributed to the absence of coal ; but this deficiency exists almost equally in Sweden, which, nevertheless, carries on a considerable and a prosperous iron industry.

The iron-ore resources of Norway are understood to be of great extent and importance.   They are mostly of the magnetic variety.   The Dunderland Iron Ore Company, constituted in this country some two or three years ago, is making plans for producing large quantities of ore on the Dunderland River for export to Great Britain, and it is more than probable that other ore-fields will by-and-by be worked for export.

RUSSIA

The Russian iron industry is one of the latest to come into prominence in Europe. Not that the industry is entirely a new one. On the contrary, it is one of the oldest of which we have reliable records, and it is well known that Russian sheet iron and bar iron have been imported into Great Britain and into other European countries for generations. It had been usual to import Russian bar iron in competition with Swedish bar iron for the purposes of the crucible-steel industry, up to at least the middle of the nineteenth century. From that date onwards Russia imported very large quantities of iron and steel from Great Britain, and in the earlier stages of the development of the Russian railway system, British rails were the chief iron imports into the empire. As the demands of the Czar's dominions increased, the iron-making resources of the country were expanded, until at the present time Russia imports relatively inconsiderable quantities of both iron and steel. The greater part of the finished material imported into Russia of late years has been received from Germany, which, on some of its frontiers, has easy access to Russian markets, and has found those markets a convenient dumping ground.

The pig-iron industry of Central Russia is the oldest of the empire. Thence it has spread to the Urals, Siberia, and later to Southern Russia. The iron trade would naturally first spring up in those districts which possessed rich deposits of iron ore, together with an abundance of wood. Central Russia embraces the governments of Tula, Kaluga, Orel, Riäsan, Vladimir, Nishni-Novgorod and Tambov. These parts formerly were well wooded and possessed an ample supply of iron ore. The blast furnaces up to the year 1897 used exclusively wood charcoal, and were therefore not dependent on any other province for their raw materials.

The iron ores smelted are brown hematite and sphero-siderite or spathic iron ore. The brown ores, which contain only a small proportion of manganese, form on the boundary of the Devonian limestone groups which are covered with deposits of sand. The area over which these ores extend is very extensive, and the numerous remains of shallow shafts, now dilapidated, bear witness to workings of former days, which as early as the seventeenth century supplied the iron-ore industry of those times. The spathic iron ore is embedded in Jura clay, and contains more than 40 per cent. of iron. The ores are extracted from a depth of from 10 to 15 metres from shafts served by a windlass. The method of obtaining the ore is still almost everywhere of a most primitive character. Generally speaking, the peasants cart the crude ore to the ironworks. Some of the principal mines opened up during recent years have been worked on more up-to-date methods, and progress is continuous.

The bicentenary jubilee of the Russian mining and metallurgical industries was celebrated on December 18th, 1900. Peter the Great was their founder, and the Urals their birthplace. The iron trade has always been pre-dominant in the Urals, and until 1804 Ural iron was exported to Germany and to England. The develop-ment of the metallurgical industries of the Urals has been a slow and lengthy one, and in this respect they differ greatly from the feverish growth of the South Russian sister trades. During the last decade, however, a notable revival has taken place : thus in 1890 the pro-duction of pig iron in the Urals was 447,000 tons, while in 1900 it had risen to over 800,000 tons. This was due to the erection of new works, and chiefly to the addition and re-erection of old blast furnaces at previously existing works, and to the general adoption of the hot blast. The average annual production per blast furnace has risen from 4,322 to 6,613 tons, and in certain cases the daily yield amounts to 50 tons on charcoal fuel alone.

The yield of pig iron in the Ural blast furnaces is about 10 tons per 9 tons of charcoal fuel consumed. There are 107 active ironworks in the district. Of these, 65 possess blast furnaces (from 1 to 4 furnaces), 39 prepare manufactured iron, 3 roll rails, 7 are engineering works, 5 gun and small-arms works, and 1 railway waggon and carriage works. The largest amount of pig iron smelted by a single works was 40,323 tons, and of manufactured iron, 22,580 tons.

The chief centre of the modern iron industry of Russia is the south, where there are now a number of works of large dimensions and more or less fully up-to-date. Some of these works severally produce over 250,000 tons of pig iron, and from 100,000 to 200,000 tons of steel per annum. The south of Russia produces hardly any iron except with mineral fuel. Ironworks are also carried on in Poland, in Finland, and in various other parts of the empire. Very heavy duties are levied on most of the iron and steel products imported.

In the early years of the nineteenth century the pig-iron output of Russia as a whole was only about 80,000 tons, and in 1850 it did not exceed 250,000 tons. In 1898, for the first time, the output exceeded 2,000,000 tons, and it is now about 3,000,000 tons annually.

Russia does a very considerable business in the mining and export of manganese ores, which are found in great abundance in the Caucasus. This is a comparatively new business, the mining of the Shorapan ores having begun only in 1879. The average annual output of these ores has advanced from 60,000 tons a year in the period

1885-7 to 145,000 tons in 1895-7, and to about 600,000 tons at the present time.

The distribution of the Caucasian manganese trade among a large number of small enterprises is a great drawback. For example, in 1899 the total production of 548,400 tons was divided among 290 firms, which, taking the average price of the ore at the mines as from 8s. 6½d. to 9s. 11d. a ton, makes from £800 to £900 for each firm. There are only ten firms producing over 160 tons, and in 1899 they raised over 25 per cent. of the total production. The result of this is that the export trade is entirely in the hands of a few commission agents, who fetter the industry considerably.

In recent years the quality of the ore delivered from the mines has deteriorated from carelessness and dishonesty, with the result that it now often contains up to 30 per cent. of rubbish. Russia is consequently gradually losing her priority in the manganese trade. Her chief rival at present is India.

The course of the iron industry in Russia during the last two years has been so unsatisfactory that very little progress has been made in extending production. The most strongly formative period in the recent history of the trade was that between 1890 and 1900, when the annual output of pig iron rose from 926,590 to 2,875,000 tons. Of this latter quantity 1,506,384 tons, or more than 50 per cent., were produced in the south by nineteen furnaces, whereas in the Urals only 802,885 tons were produced by ninety-five furnaces—nearly all charcoal. In 1901 and 1902 the output of Russian pig iron fell below the output of 1900.

Russia now produces about 85 per cent. of her total requirements in iron and steel. Indeed, for the last two years the imports of all kinds of both metals have not much exceeded 300,000 tons a year. Germany has in recent years taken a stronger position in the Russian markets than formerly, but only for a time.

AUSTRIA-HUNGARY

The antiquity of the iron trade of Austria may be inferred from the fact that the country claims the doubtful distinction of having manufactured the nails which were used to nail Jesus Christ to the cross. It is certain that the industry is of very great antiquity, especially in the two provinces of Styria and Carinthia, aided by the remarkably pure deposits of iron ore found in the Styrian Alps. The steel industry was of greater importance in Austria half a century ago than in any other European country except Great Britain. In 1854 the total output of Austrian steel was reported at 13,037 tons. Within ten years of the adoption of the Bessemer process in England the Austrians had fourteen Bessemer converters at work, producing, however, only 650 tons of steel weekly. The Bessemer process was introduced into Hungary in 1867 at the works of Resicza.

The Austrian iron and steel industries do not call here for much notice, since they have comparatively little international importance. Until about sixteen years ago they were mainly limited to half a dozen establishments, largely controlled by the *Alpine Montan Gesellschaft*, which also controlled the great bulk of the ore supplies of the Styrian Erzberg. Within the last few years—thanks mainly to the enterprise of Mr. Karl Wittgenstein, of Vienna—the works of this company have been largely remodelled, and some of the newer plants, such as those of Kladno and Donawitz, are equal to the best in Europe. A very fine plant is also engaged at Trieste making pig iron from Spanish ores and Durham coke.

Hungary, like Austria, has also achieved the distinction of considerable antiquity as an iron-producing country, but the modern plants are few, and the total output of pig iron does not much exceed half a million tons a year. Until within the last quarter of a century iron was the product mainly turned out. There are now some half a dozen steel-producing plants in Hungary, which, although not capable of competing with the newer and more up-to-date plants in the more western nations of Europe, are yet equal to supplying practically all the commercial needs of this part of the dual kingdom.

The total output of pig iron in Austria-Hungary is about 1½ million tons a year, and the output of steel is well over a million tons a year. A speciality of the Austrian iron trade is the manufacture of malleable iron castings, and another is that of agricultural and horticultural implements, especially sickles, of which large quantities are exported.

SPAIN

Hitherto Spain has chiefly figured in the ironmaking world as a "hewer of wood and a drawer of water" to other countries. In other words, Spanish ore has been the alimony whereby the steel industry of other European countries has been maintained. The export of such ores has been steadily increasing from year to year for more than thirty years past, and has risen to fully nine million tons a year. Much the greater part of this large supply has been furnished by the district of Bilbao, in the northern province of Biscay, but within recent years, ores of iron have been worked in considerable quantities in the more southerly provinces, on the Mediterranean, and Almeria, Cartagena, Malaga, and other ports on the littoral now provide Great Britain, Germany, and France with notable and increasing quantities of high-class ores, suited to the production of Bessemer or open-hearth steel of the acid variety. Most of the British works that produce this steel

H

are interested in Spanish ore mines, including firms in Cleveland, Wales, Scotland, Cumberland, and elsewhere. The total annual quantity of British pig iron made from Spanish ores over the last ten years may be taken at nearly three million tons, or considerably over one-third of our total annual output.

The iron-ore resources of Spain are in some districts becoming rapidly depleted, and it is some years since the reserves of the Bilbao district were computed at less than ten years' supply at the recent rate of exhaustion. This estimate was probably true as regards the original sources of supply, but considerable additional resources have become available outside the original radius, and it is now probable that these will maintain the output for a considerably longer period. In other provinces, and especially those of Murcia, Andalusia, and Leon, there are still vast deposits of iron ore that have hardly as yet been touched.[1]

The iron ores of Bilbao have, during the period of their working, been placed f.o.b. in the Bilbao River at 5s. to 10s. per ton, according to the character of the demand, the cost of labour, and kindred conditions. The freight to England has ranged from 4s. to 7s. per ton, according to the same fluctuating elements of cost. The cost of the Bilbao ore delivered in an English port has ranged from 10s. 6d. to 20s. per ton, a fair average of the last few years being about 15s. per ton. The best ore runs about 50 per cent. of iron, so that two tons are required to produce one ton of pig iron.

Spain has, during the last quarter of a century, erected and worked various plants for the production of pig iron, Bessemer and open-hearth steel, and tin-plates, while there are a number of small plants here and there engaged in

A valuable monograph on the iron ore of Leon has recently been published by my friend Julio de Lazurtigui of Bilbao, which places the reserves of that province at 150,000,000 tons.

the manufacture of finished iron. The most important plants in all categories are in the province of Biscay. The annual output of pig iron is about 300,000 tons, while that of steel is not more than 200,000 tons. Spain has not yet reached the point of supplying all domestic needs, but this fact does not appear to stand in the way of a limited export trade being done in both iron and steel. Indeed, it has been estimated that Spain should be able to produce pig iron as cheaply as any country in Europe. A fair estimate of cost at Bilbao will be approximately as under :—

	£	s.	d.
Two tons of Rubio ore at 8s. .	0	16	0
One ton of coke at 20s.	1	0	0
Half a ton limestone at 3s.	0	1	6
Labour and incidentals	0	5	0
Total cost per ton of pig iron .	2	2	6

In cases where pig-iron-makers have their own mines, the cost of ore should be less, and something may be gained by using local coke, which, however, is of poor quality.

OTHER COUNTRIES

Among other ironmaking countries, progress has recently been made in Italy, Bosnia, Japan, and China, but the quantity produced in each case is still small and entirely non-competitive. The total of such output is not likely to exceed half a million tons annually.

CHAPTER X

SOME PROMINENT CONDITIONS OF THE BRITISH IRON TRADE

CAPITALISATION

THERE are a number of features of the iron trade of Great Britain that have not hitherto been dealt with, although they exercise a material influence on its circumstances and outlook. Some of those features are more or less shared by other countries. Others are special to the British iron industry. The latter appear to call for priority of attention.

The first of these features is that of the competitive situation of the British iron trade in respect of raw material, labour, transport, and tariff systems. Most of these, and kindred matters, are separately considered. But we may here take up with advantage a few ancillary and collateral aspects of the trade, beginning with that of capital expenditure.

There is no record of the capital expenditure in the iron trade of Great Britain as a whole, nor is there too much information on this aspect of the subject for any other country. The census returns of the United States do present every ten years statements of the actual or computed capital embarked in the various branches of the trade; but even in the case of statistics so collected, and so originating, there is grave reason for doubting the validity and accuracy of the figures. There is in most American industries a notable tendency to over-capitalise. That tendency is not unknown in Europe. In some German works and mines it has been carried very far. In Great Britain there is a liability to two extremes—to under-capitalise, as in the case of the Consett Iron Company, whose valuable coal and iron ore properties were purchased for much less than their actual normal value, and as in the case of the Dowlais Iron Company, whose vast mineral and manufacturing properties were purchased by their present owners for much less than they had actually cost; or to over-capitalise, as in the case of a number of concerns, of which Barrow, whose original capital has had to be largely written down, may perhaps be taken as a type.

Obviously the correct standard of capitalisation for a property producing minerals is the total reserve and output which the capital represents, and for ironmaking or steel-manufacturing properties, the standard is, or should be, the productive capacity of the plants employed.

I have taken some trouble to ascertain what this standard is and should be in relation to various products. The ratio varies greatly in various districts and in different works and plants. Speaking generally, a coal property should not produce less than one ton per annum for every 20s. invested. This is perhaps as near a normal figure as can be got in the case of blast furnace plants, and more often than not it will be found that, in this country at all events, a blast furnace that has cost £30,000 should be capable of producing about 30,000 tons a year. In steel properties the range is very wide. Much depends upon the product. In order to produce ordinary merchant steel, from 25s. to 30s. of capital per ton of annual product is not likely to be far from the normal, but of course it varies within considerable limits, according to the period, the district, and the conditions under which the installation was carried out.

No guidance on this matter can be got from the published figures of syndicated capitalisation. The United States Steel Corporation, for example, have a ridiculously small output of both iron and steel in relation to their capital. Their maximum capacity of pig-iron output may be 12,000,000 tons, and of steel output it may be 13,000,000 tons, while the actual capacity of the output of minerals of all kinds, including coal and iron ore, will not be short of 45,000,000 tons, of which fully 20,000,000 tons will be iron ores. Here we have a total capacity of 70,000,000 tons, up to and including the cruder forms of steel. To convert these cruder forms into fully finished forms, the capital apportioned to steel plants would perhaps have to be doubled. This would raise the capitalisation to approximately £85,000,000 sterling. But the actual capitalisation of the Steel Corporation is close on £300,000,000 sterling, which means considerably more than £3 of capital per ton of output. This fact does not in any way disturb the relevancy of the standards we have assumed, because, in the first place, the Corporation is generally understood to have been over-capitalised to the extent of well on to twice the original value of the plants acquired ; and, in the second place, the Corporation properties include such adjuncts as docks, railways, ore-carrying steamers, etc., which are not all necessarily used in an ironmaking business.

PUBLIC BURDENS

The British iron industry is increasingly handicapped by public burdens, and more especially by those that belong to local and imperial taxation, of which this great business necessarily pays a large share. Of these two categories of burdens, local rates are the most severely felt. A recent return shows that the local loans have risen from £198,000,000 in 1890 to £293,000,000 in 1900, an

increase of 47·9 per cent. The services chiefly responsible
for the increase have been as follows :—

Services.	1890. £		1900. £		Increase per cent.
Education	. 18,240,088	...	30,269,534	...	65·9
Sewage	. 19,352,382	...	29,326,175	...	51·5
Poor Law and Hospitals	7,037,304	...	10,893,293	...	54·7
Highways	. 28,828,949	...	35,932,202	...	24·6
Lunacy	. 3,557,436	...	6,320,140	...	13·7
Gasworks	. 14,851,731	...	19,819,301	...	33·4
Waterworks	. 37,730,323	...	53,404,347	...	41·5
Tramways	. 1,276,410	...	5,776,147	...	352·5
Harbours, Piers, etc.	. 31,114,487	...	36,745,397	...	18·0
Parks	. 3,743,387	...	5,936,059	...	58·5

The expenditure on electric lighting, not shown ten
years ago, is now £7,853,000. In ten years there has
been an increase of £2,000,000 on public offices. Smaller
increases are spread over a number of purposes, many of
them relating to services of recent creation. Under the
present system of granting loans only for short periods,
an excessive charge is placed on present ratepayers for
work which will benefit future generations.

During the same ten years the total expenditure of all
local authorities in Great Britain has increased by 46·4
per cent. from public rates and by 72·9 per cent. from
imperial grants, while the increase in loans has been not
less than 276·7 per cent. The average rates have in this
period increased from 3s. 8d. to 4s. 11½d. in the £.

Other burdens that have been levied on the trade
during recent years have been the direct consequence of
legislative interference, which threatens every year to
make manufacturing industry more onerous. Among
such burdens, that imposed by the Employers' Liability
and Workmen's Compensation Acts may be cited as
typical.

MINERAL ROYALTIES

It has not infrequently been argued that one main reason of the relative decline of the British iron industry is the existence of a system of high royalty rents, which compare unfavourably with the kindred circumstances of other countries. It is true that the cases in which minerals are worked free from royalty rents are comparatively few, but that is chiefly because those who work the minerals have only in comparatively few cases taken steps to secure the freehold. The royalties paid in respect of most minerals worked under the same and similar conditions are quite as high in the United States as in this country, with very few exceptions. The coal royalties there are lower than here, but so also is the value of coal. A Royal Commission which sat on this question nearly twenty years ago presented some interesting conclusions as to the amount of royalties paid on the working of British minerals. The most important of these conclusions was that the average British iron-ore royalty was about 9d. per ton, while the average coal royalty was taken at about 5d. per ton. These figures, calculated on the British output of iron ores and coal in 1901, would give a total royalty payment of about £4,600,000 for coal, and £450,000 for iron ores, or a total for both descriptions of mineral of £5,050,000. In addition to this, there is a considerable, though relatively insignificant, payment on both minerals in respect of way-leaves—that is to say, the liberty to move mineral traffic over another person's land in order to reach a railway line or a shipping port—which was given as about £202,000 for coal and £14,781 for iron ores.

Some recent writers and speakers have declared that this country has reached the maximum of its producing capacity. This view appears to have been taken by

Mr. Carnegie, and by Dr. Jacks, of Glasgow, among others. If the conclusion be founded on British ores alone, it may be near the truth. But if we can produce, as we now do, between three and four million tons of pig iron annually, from imported ores, why should we not produce very much more? This is almost a recent feature of the trade. A quarter of a century ago our iron output was practically entirely from home ores. New sources of suitable foreign supplies would be likely to give an impetus to increased production. At the same time it appears to be probable that there would be greater rivalry to possess any such supplies in the future than there has been in the past, so that this element of cost would be likely to be greater.

STANDING CHARGES

In the iron trade, as in other branches of commerce, the costs of production are divisible under the heads of raw materials, labour, depreciation, and standing charges. The item of standing charges is usually the most elastic and difficult to regulate. The principal items included under this head are clerical charges, rates and taxes, interest on capital, agencies, advertising, and administration. It is of the utmost importance, in any branch of manufacture, that these charges should be spread over as large an output as possible. The most effective method of keeping down standing charges is to keep a plant fully employed. If works are kept going full time during the whole twenty-four hours, the standing charges of interest, rates, taxes, etc., should be even less than one-half what they would be if the plant were kept going only twelve hours. Standing charges vary greatly, according to the commodity and its production. In this country they are generally more per ton of product than in Germany or America, because the Germans and Americans make great efforts to run full time, and in order to do this they do not hesitate to sell their surplus in foreign markets at a very low figure.

STANDARD SPECIFICATIONS AND SECTIONS

Until within the last few years, one of the greatest disabilities of the iron trade of the United Kingdom was our relatively old-fashioned methods of providing for the manufacture and supply of sections of iron and steel, and the variety of specifications and tests made use of. This had for many years been felt to be a grievance, alike by manufacturers, merchants, engineers, and the general public. When both the United States and Germany determined to adopt standard specifications and sections, the grievance became intolerable. It was possible for any consulting engineer to recommend and to insist on the adoption of almost any kind of specification and section he liked. Every engineer had his own preferences, and they were often, if not generally, pushed to the extremest limits, regardless of the cost, trouble, and inconvenience involved. Works that were largely engaged in the manufacture of girders, beams, pillars, angles, and other sectional material, had not only to keep very large stocks of rolls, suited to the caprices of the customers for whom they worked, and of their inspecting engineers, but they had often to undertake the cost and the trouble of having entirely new rolls, unnecessarily cut to suit new caprices. This condition of affairs was all the more lamentable that it had largely been remedied in both Germany and the United States, so that Great Britain was, in the cost of sections involving special rolls, etc., placed at a disadvantage compared with those countries, even where, as often happened, the buyer had to pay the piper. The American manufacturer, with a set of standard sections, was able to say, and generally did say, to a customer who ordered a section not on the standard list, "We don't roll that section, but if you pay the cost of a new set of rolls" —which sometimes cost over three thousand dollars— "and give us a sufficiently large order to make a reasonable run, we will take it up."[1] When the customer ascertained that the standard sections covered practically all reasonable requirements, and that any other section involved considerable additional cost, he generally fell in with the arrangement most convenient to the manufacturer, and cheapest to himself. Yet it was not until 1895 that a successful effort was made, even in the United States, to use standard specifications for iron and steel, nor was it until June, 1898, that the formation of the American Section of the International Association for testing materials enabled those concerned to come together and frame standard specifications covering the various categories of iron and steel products, which, after much discussion, were finally adopted in June, 1901.

While this was the situation in the United States, the British Iron Trade Association had its attention called to the importance of the whole question, as affecting the British iron and steel industries; and in May, 1900, at a Conference held in London, at which certain details were put forward in a paper read by Mr. H. J. Skelton, it was resolved to take steps to secure the co-operation of the various technical societies, and others concerned, to bring about a reduction in the number of sections, and improvements in the specifications and tests adopted.

The Association learned that in the steelworks of Great Britain there were nearly five times the number of sections of angles, tees, joists, zeds, etc., rolled that there were in the leading steelworks of the United States. To keep so large a number of sections on the section books of

[1] See my Report, as an American Commissioner, on *American Industrial Conditions and Competition*, p. 256.

steel-manufacturing firms was stated to involve a great deal of expenditure, and there were works, of which particulars had been obtained, where the first cost of the rolls used was not less than £35,000.

In August the Board sent out circular letters to the trade in order to ascertain the views of manufacturers and societies as to the adoption of standard sections.

So far as replies were received from the engineering and kindred societies whose co-operation had been invited, the response made from that direction was favourable. In order to ascertain the views of steel manufacturers, blank forms were issued, which elicited a practically unanimous response in favour of standard sections. The movement was facilitated by the appointment, subsequent to the action taken by the Association, of a committee of the Institution of Civil Engineers to deal with the whole question. On that committee three important members of the British Iron Trade Association were elected. Meanwhile, a special committee of the British Iron Trade Association, appointed in the early part of 1901 to deal with this question, had it under consideration, and arrangements were made to prepare a provisional list of standard sections, and afterwards to have that list submitted to and discussed by the Standard Sections Committee of the Institution of Civil Engineers.[1]

This is hardly the time or place to enter into a discussion of the rival claims of different organisations to have originated and carved out a great public movement, attended with enormous advantage to those interests that were primarily concerned ; but it may at least be stated that it was unquestionably the British Iron Trade Association that initiated this great movement, and called the attention of the various technical societies to its importance, while it was reserved for those societies, acting collectively,

[1] Report of Board, June 14th, 1901.

to provide the machinery whereby the movement was carried to the successful issue which it has since attained.

THROUGH RATES

Another considerable disability from which the British iron trade has hitherto suffered, is that due to inadequate arrangements to quote through ocean and rail rates to all the important markets of the world. The Americans appear to have mastered this branch of transportation much better than the British. At any rate, complaints are continually being made that the British manufacturer and merchant does not possess the same facilities for through freight rates as his rivals. The result of such a want is that orders that would otherwise be placed are withheld in the absence of definite knowledge as to what the final cost at the place of delivery is likely to be. Much of the success of the United States and Germany in foreign markets is attributed to the great care which they have taken to secure the lowest possible rates of freight, and the exactness of the information they are able to give as to the ultimate price to be paid. The foreign shipper has several things in his favour if he knows how to take advantage of them. He has first the element of competition of one country against another; next, the competition of the ports for shipping; and, finally, the eagerness of both home and foreign railways to increase their traffic, and especially traffic which does not originate on their own systems, and is, therefore, not necessarily secure. During the sittings of the Industrial Commission of the United States some years ago, the representatives of the railroads who were examined regarding this discrimination attributed the low through rates for imported goods to the competition of the ports for shipping. The steamship lines make a rate to secure the business, and the railroad companies co-operate with them, even though the proportion received for the rail haul is less than the regular rail tariff.

SHIPPING "CONFERENCES"

The prevalence and the power of so-called shipping conferences are a serious drawback to British business in certain important markets, and especially those of South Africa, Australasia, and India. These conferences are designed to secure that traders are more or less absolutely at the mercy of the principal steamship lines serving those countries. Those lines arrange to allow a drawback, usually of 10 per cent., to firms shipping their goods entirely by them, but this rebate is retained for a long time, as a pledge of the loyal behaviour of the shipper, and is entirely confiscated if he departs in any way from the terms on which it is granted. Hence, shippers are often unable, even if they greatly wish it, to ship by any other than the regular and more or less monopolistic shipping companies. The case is made much worse for British trade by the lower rates of freight at the disposal of foreign rivals, who are not subject to such tyranny.

The following table of ocean freight rates shows that though the distance from this country to Cape Town is less than that from America, the freights charged for some classes of iron goods are greatly more than those paid from the United States to Cape Town :—

Article.	From U.K. Distance 6,181 miles.		From U.S.A. Distance 6,800 miles.	
	s.	d.	s.	d.
Cement	16	3	15	0
Bricks	22	6	15	0
Deals	20	0	15	0
Galvanised Iron	20	0	15	0
Bar Iron	22	6	15	0

In America the freights are under the wholesome check of real competition, because the "ring" has not been able to get rid of the rivalry of the Prince Line ; but hitherto the "Conference" has been able to smother every attempt at competition here. The last effort of the kind was made in 1903 by Messrs. R. P. Houston & Co., but at a later date the Cape Shipping Conference notified in a circular that the "rate war" was ended, that Messrs. Houston would in future co-operate with the Conference, and that the cheaper rates which had for a short time been in force would be withdrawn.

WATERWAYS AND RAILWAYS

Still another disability of the British iron industry is the very limited amount of the competition, both absolutely and relatively, which waterways offer to railways. The total amount of mineral traffic carried on British canals does not exceed 30,500,000 tons, although we have a total system that approximates 4,000 miles. In Germany, France, and one or two other continental countries, the canal traffic is relatively greater, and so in the United States, with its river traffic on the Ohio, the Mississippi, the Missouri, the Hudson, and other rivers, as well as the great lakes. The greatest traffic carried on any English waterway is rather over four million tons, carried on the Birmingham canals.

CHAPTER XI

TRANSPORTATION OF IRONMAKING MATERIALS

THE iron and steel trades are more dependent for their success or failure upon railway facilities and conditions than most other businesses. A blast furnace of up-to-date capacity will consume an average of perhaps 3,500 tons of iron ore, 1,500 tons of coke, and 500 tons of limestone, per week. It will produce 1,500 tons of pig iron and 1,500 to 2,000 tons of slag in the same time. All this material has to be handled by railway for either long or short distances. If the distances are long, and the rates high, the chances of the business being carried on with a profit are much less than they would be with shorter distances and lower rates.

What is known as the cost of assembling materials varies greatly as between different countries and different districts in the same country. There are comparatively few districts and hardly any countries where the materials lie "within a ring fence" to any extent. All the great ironmaking countries import considerable quantities of iron ore, or of coke, or of both, to supplement their own home supplies. No country is more independent of outside supplies than the United States, and yet the blast furnaces on the Atlantic seaboard import from half a million to a million and a half tons of iron ore annually. Germany imports four to five million tons of ore annually; France, two to three million tons; Belgium, nearly two million

ARMOUR PLATE SHOPS AT RIVER DON WORKS

tons; Austria-Hungary, well on to half a million tons; and Great Britain, six to seven million tons annually.

Some other countries import considerable quantities of coke. In this category are included France, Spain, Austria, Germany, Belgium, Sweden, and Italy. Great Britain imports neither coal nor coke on a commercial scale.

Apart from the importance of cheap transport to countries that import large quantities of raw material, there is also to be considered, as more or less determining factors, the conditions and costs of local transport within the country itself. In some cases distances are long and railway charges are low. In other cases distances are short and railway charges are high. Some districts, such as Cleveland in our own country, and the Alabama iron-making region in the United States, have all the necessary minerals within a radius of twenty miles more or less; while others, such as the Pittsburg district in the United States, the Loire district in France, the Westphalian district in Germany, and the South Wales district in Great Britain, have to bring their materials, either as fuel or as ore, very long distances.

The cost of long transport, under the conditions of fifty years ago, would have rendered it impossible to make pig iron at present-day prices with a profit. When the Lake Superior iron-ore region was first opened up, it cost 25s. to 30s. per ton to transport the ore from there to Pittsburg, the principal centre of consumption. The same service has since been rendered over long periods for less than 6s. per ton, including two breakages of bulk and two railway transports—the distance being approximately a thousand miles. Iron ore is carried from Spain to Glasgow, Newport, Cardiff, and other English ports, a distance varying from 800 to 1,000 miles, for 4s. to 5s. per ton; and other water freights are almost equally low.

I

This is more especially true as regards internal transport of the canal and river rates paid in Germany, France, and Belgium, as one notable example of which the Rhine freights from Rotterdam to Westphalia may be quoted, the distance being several hundred miles, and the cost only about a shilling a ton. Great Britain, both in respect to water transport and in respect to land carriage, has to pay higher freight rates than competitive nations, but against this she has some advantage in generally shorter hauls.

The cost of fuel at the pit's mouth is about the same in Germany and in Great Britain; in the United States it is 1s. to 2s. per ton cheaper; and in France and Belgium it is 1s. to 1s. 6d. per ton dearer. The conditions of distance already referred to modify these values at works in relation to the length of haul, which may be taken at approximately the following rates of freight per ton of coal or coke :—

GREAT BRITAIN.

	s. d.		s. d.
Cleveland . .	2 0	to	3 0
Cumberland . .	7 0	,,	7 6
South Wales . .	1 0	,,	1 6
Scotland . .	1 0	,,	1 6
Lincolnshire . .	4 0	,,	5 0
Northamptonshire .	5 0	,,	6 0
South Staffordshire .	1 0	,,	1 6

UNITED STATES.

	s. d.		s. d.
Pittsburg . .	3 0	to	4 0
Alabama . .	1 6	,,	2 0
Valley furnaces .	4 0		

GERMANY.

	s. d.		s. d.
Westphalia . .	1 6	,,	2 0
Lorraine . .	6 0	,,	7 0
Luxemburg . .	6 0	,,	7 0

In most other districts the costs of transport per ton of pig iron generally take a higher range than those of Cleveland, except at a few of the Scotch works where the local ore is still used, and in which the coal and the ironstone are practically mined on the spot. Nevertheless, the distances to be covered are not in any case such as would be considered excessive, but rather the contrary, in any other country except our own. It is probable that the district of South Staffordshire labours under greater disadvantages than any other, since the local supplies of iron ore are limited, and by no means cheap, while the markets for a large part of the finished products, although geographically close at hand, are, in point of cost, a long way off. There is no important centre of the American iron industry that would not be regarded as admirably situated for foreign trade if located as near to the sea as this district. No such good fortune, however, attends the American iron trade. Even in the neighbourhood of Philadelphia the ironworks are over a hundred miles from the ocean, while in Pittsburg they are nearly 500 miles, in Chicago nearly 1,000 miles, and in Cleveland, Ohio, and Youngstown (Ohio), they are 550 to 600 miles.

It would naturally be supposed that in a small country like Great Britain, with no point of its area more than a hundred miles or so from a seaport, the cost of transport would be much less than in countries which, like Germany and the United States, are differently situated. Geographical conditions should be entirely favourable to this country.

But the natural advantages of our geographical position are not realised as they should be, because of the relatively high railway rates enforced and the absence of competition. In America, railway rates per ton-mile are from one-half to one-third of their general level in this country. The general average for mineral transport in Great Britain is probably $1d.$ per ton-mile, the average haul being from twenty to thirty miles. In the United States the average mineral rate is from $\frac{1}{4}d.$ to $\frac{1}{3}d.$, the average haul being about 110 miles. When we compare short hauls, the differences are not so marked.

The following are some of the actual rates now or recently quoted for the transportation from three leading stations in the Staffordshire district to some of the leading centres of consumption and export of bars, hoops, and sheets, the chief products of the Staffordshire mills and forges :—

To			Rates per ton. s.	d.	To			Rates per ton. s.	d.
Glasgow	.	.	20	0	Workington	.	.	16	8
Durham	.	.	18	4	Carlisle	.	.	17	6
Hull .	.	.	13	4	Huddersfield	.	.	11	8
London	.	.	15	0	Liverpool	.	.	10	0
Newcastle	.	.	18	4	Cardiff	.	.	9	2
Preston	.	.	12	6					

These rates are quoted for two-ton lots, and are un-damageable, the damageable rate being about 2s. 6d. per ton more, and four-ton lots and upwards costing usually about 2s. 6d. per ton less. The average rate throughout varies from 1¼d. to 1½d. per ton per mile. The average rate under as similar conditions as it would be possible to obtain in the United States would be less than a halfpenny per ton per mile, and in not a few competitive cases it would be little over a farthing; in Germany it would be from ½d. to ¾d.; and in Belgium, for export purposes, it would be nearly four-tenths of a penny. The very cheapest rate at which Staffordshire iron can reach a port appears to be about 8s. per ton, which is the rate quoted for four-ton lots and upwards to Liverpool, whereas Carnegie's can send finished steel of the same description from Pittsburg to New York, a distance of 460 miles, for 6s. 6d. to 8s.; the Tennessee Iron Company can send pig iron from Tennessee and Alabama to Mobile, over 260 miles, for about 4s.; and Cockerills, of Belgium, can send finished iron and steel to Antwerp or Terneuzen, distances of 80 and 106 miles, respectively, for less than a halfpenny per ton per mile for lots of five tons. Again, the Germans can send finished iron and steel from the centre of Westphalia to Amsterdam, a distance of 147 miles, for 6s. 4d.; to Rotterdam, a distance of 156 miles, for 6s. 7d.; and to Antwerp, a distance of 173 miles, for

7s. 6d. per ton, special rates on a lower scale being often quoted.

So far as the future is concerned, it appears to be highly probable that reductions of rates may come into effect in this country, as the result of introducing economies in methods and conditions of working heavy traffic. The adoption of all-steel waggons, the use of heavier rolling stock, the general running of heavier train-loads, and other changes conformable to up-to-date American and German railway practice should enable British railway companies to reduce materially their present maximum rates and charges.

It would be uncandid to ignore the fact that British conditions do not lend themselves to low ton-mile rates to the same extent as those of Continental countries and the United States—first, because of the shorter haul and relatively high terminal charges; next, because of the much higher cost of railway construction in this country; and finally because of differences in the conditions and methods of handling the traffic. It is to be feared that some of these differences against British railway transport are irremediable.

CHAPTER XII

LABOUR CONDITIONS AND REMUNERATION

IN an industry whose circumstances are liable to such serious and constant fluctuations as that of the manufacture of iron and steel, labour conditions must necessarily vary greatly between one period and another. These changes have, however, mostly been limited to the steel branch of the industry. Great changes have undoubtedly taken place in the pig-iron branch of the industry, but on the whole the cost of producing pig iron has not, in Great Britain at least, greatly altered during the last fifty years. At any rate, it is more than fifty years since Messrs. Bolckow and Vaughan stated that they were able to produce pig iron at Middlesbrough for less than 30s. per ton, and it is doubtful if during the last thirty years that figure has been improved upon. In the case of the mining of iron ore and coal, and in that of producing coke, the recent changes, although both numerous and important, have not, on the whole, enabled a cheaper product to be obtained, or, to put it with more exactness, any differences tending to a reduction of cost have been more than countervailed by other differences tending to increase that cost. The methods whereby iron ore and coal are mined, coke is manufactured, and pig iron is produced, are in all essential details the same as those that prevailed half a century ago. Economies have no doubt been adopted as the result of utilising waste gases, increasing the capacity and the blowing power of blast furnaces, the use of more effective and economical blowing engines, hot-blast stoves, and other features of equipment, but the average cost of making pig iron, owing to the great increase of other charges, has not been greatly reduced.

It has been quite otherwise with the steel industry, which within the same period has been the sport of frequent changes that have mostly been of a revolutionary character, and the net result of which has been, to use Mr. Carnegie's phrase, to enable three ounces of that product to be sold for a penny! This wonderful result has been accomplished not by a concurrent reduction, but by a great all-round increase in the wages paid to the workmen employed, not in one country only, but in all countries alike.

The extent to which the efficiency of labour has been increased in the iron trade has been very remarkable, and great as have been the similar changes in other manufacturing industries, there are few, if any, that can present a parallel. Although, as I have just indicated, there have been but few epoch-making revolutions during recent years, affecting mining or the production of pig iron, yet some figures placed at my disposal show that in respect of a large output in both categories the following results have happened in one of the greatest centres of the European iron industry :—

Tons of Annual Output of Iron Ore per Workman Employed

1880.		1902.		Increase in 1902.
200	...	430	...	230

Tons of Pig Iron Produced per Worker at Blast Furnaces

1880.		1902.		Increase in 1902.
130	...	370	...	240

These differences are typical, and represent neither maxima nor minima. The former must be sought for in some of the great Pittsburg works, where the average output of a blast furnace is often maintained at over 600 tons per day, and it is probable that the minimum of change would be found at some British works, carried on in the Midlands, whose conditions have hardly undergone alteration for many years, unless it be that of the substitution of closed for open tops, and the adoption of hot-blast firebrick stoves.

The improvements affecting labour that have been introduced into the steel industry may be estimated by one or two figures borrowed from the carefully kept records of the German iron trade, which extend backwards for about sixty years. These show that while in the year 1853—three years before the Bessemer process was introduced—the average annual output of steel per workman was only 7 tons, the average had in 1880 increased to 30 tons, and in 1902 to 54 tons. In the manufacture of foundry products the annual German average per worker was 14·3 tons in 1880 and 20·2 tons in 1902.

While in all countries alike there has been a great increase of the average productiveness of labour over the last twenty-five years, this advance has been more especially marked in the United States, where the average annual output of pig iron per employee in 1870 was only 66 tons, compared with 80·6 tons in 1880 and 370 tons in 1900.

The numbers of hands employed in four of the principal centres of the British iron and steel industries in the census year 1900 were as under :—

District or County.	Blast furnaces.		Puddling furnaces and rolling mills.		Steelworks— melting and founding.
Durham . .	1,828	...	3,033	...	3,524
Yorkshire .	3,564	...	7,783	...	13,354
Lancashire .	1,313	...	3,765	...	2,052
Glamorganshire	363	...	935	...	3,415

The Yorkshire figures include all parts of the county, and, therefore, embrace both Sheffield and Middlesbrough. They also, of course, embrace all branches of the steel trade—crucible, Bessemer, and open-hearth. The entry of puddling furnaces and rolling mills under one head is unfortunate, as it renders it impossible to separate the numbers employed at puddling furnaces from those employed in totally different plants and in a totally different branch of the trade—*i.e.* rolling mills.

The other principal centres of the trade are the Midlands, Scotland, and West Cumberland.

The question of the relation of wages to product and to other conditions of manufacture is a very complex one, and this complexity is liable to lead to confusion and error. So far as I know, no general attempt has ever been made to arrive at the average wages paid at iron and steel works in this country. Some years ago, however, I had occasion to get from some leading British works details of the total and average amount of wages paid, and the results came out as follows :—

	Average annual wages.
	£
Yorkshire, steelworks only	70
Lancashire, iron and steel works . .	79
Do. do. do. . .	71
Derbyshire, blast furnaces and foundries .	60
Northamptonshire, blast furnaces . .	64
South Wales, steelworks only . . .	75
West Cumberland, blast furnaces . .	66
South Staffordshire, blast furnaces . .	60

The differences here shown are attributable partly to the class of labour employed, partly to the character of the locality, and to other considerations which vary in other countries much as they do in our own.

The returns affecting American wages are more full and

complete than those available for Great Britain. I have compiled the following statement from the official census returns of the United States in order to show the differences of average wages in the principal steel-manufacturing States. It will be noted that Illinois stood highest in 1890, and Ohio in 1900.

United States.—Rolling Mills and Steelworks in 1890 *and* 1900—*Numbers Employed and Average Wages Paid*

	1890.			1900.		
STATE.	No. employed.	Wages paid. 1=1,000 Dols.	Average annual wages. Dols.	No. employed.	Wages paid. 1=1,000 Dols.	Average annual wages. Dols.
Pennsylvania .	76,609	42,356	552	94,664	53,817	568
Ohio .	19,489	11,405	585	27,638	16,443	594
Illinois .	7,265	4,324	595	13,632	7,464	547
New Jersey .	4,498	2,301	511	7,699	3,600	467
Massachusetts .	5,168	2,454	475	6,099	3,401	557
Alabama .	1,696	682	462	2,204	1,072	486
West Virginia .	3,346	1,552	434	3,975	2,066	519

The tendency of wages in the United States has been to increase for many years past, but in some States the increase has been much greater than in others. A comparison of the census returns of the total wages paid to the total hands employed in each of the census years—1890 and 1900—shows that the average annual wages paid in those years in the principal States engaged in the iron industry were :—

	Average wages paid in Steelworks.	
	1890. Dollars.	1900. Dollars.
Pennsylvania . .	552 ...	562
Ohio . .	585 ...	594
Illinois . .	595 ...	547
Alabama . .	462 ...	486
W. Virginia . .	434 ...	519

The average range of American wages since the census year, 1900, is more or less imperfectly indicated by the figures published by the United States Steel Corporation, which show for all their vast properties an average of 720 dollars annually, or (converting the dollar at 4s.) about £144 per worker in mining, manufacturing, and transportation. This is almost twice the average of British works and mines, so far as I can get at it.

The President of the Federal Steel Company—now one of the constituents of the United States Steel Corporation —submitted to the Industrial Commission of that country a statement of a number of skilled and unskilled workmen employed by that company in October, 1898, and in August, 1899, from which it appeared that of the total *personnel* 34 per cent. were skilled and 45 per cent. unskilled, while within this interval the number of skilled labourers had increased by 15·97, against an increase of 22·3 per cent. in common labour. When I add that the average daily wage paid to skilled labour in 1899 was 2·53 dollars, and of unskilled labour was only 1·70 dollars, the economic importance of this differentiation becomes at once apparent. In the case of this particular company, the actual wages of unskilled labour were about £52 a year less than those of skilled workmen, and this amount, spread over a considerable number of workmen, is likely to make a vast difference in the financial results of any industry in the course of a year.

German labour has probably increased of late years, as measured by nominal wages, a good deal more than the labour employed in Great Britain. When, as one of a Commission appointed by the British Iron Trade Association, I went over the leading German works in 1895, I was surprised to find how near the wages paid in both iron and steel works came to those paid in Great

Britain. In not a few cases the rates for the same classes of work were approximately on all fours.

No reference to the circumstances of labour in the iron trade would be at all satisfactory that did not recognise the great value of the arrangements made for submitting, through conciliation, to arbitration, the disputes occurring between employers and employed which have prevailed in the North of England, and in the Midlands, since the year 1866. In that year there was a serious strike of ironworkers in the North of England, extending over many weeks, and inflicting the most serious injury on business generally. When it was ended, Mr. (now Sir) David Dale suggested the formation of a Board of Conciliation and Arbitration, with a view to the avoidance of such disputes in the future. Mr. Dale's idea was adopted, and it is not too much to say that the immunity from any general strike of iron and steel workers which we have now enjoyed in this country for more than a quarter of a century has been due partly to the prudence and sweet reasonableness of the employers, led by such men as Sir Benjamin Hingley, Sir David Dale, and Mr. William Whitwell, and partly to the strong common sense and wisdom of the workmen's representatives.

In no industry with which I am acquainted have such boards won so great triumphs over so long a period. This is no mere accident of the character of the work, which is exceedingly laborious, and taxes both the physical and the mental powers of the selected workmen to an unusual degree. We have within recent recollection had great labour conflicts in the United States, leading to riot and bloodshed. In both France and Germany labour disputes in the iron industry are not infrequent.

CHAPTER XIII

HOME MARKETS AND SOURCES OF DEMAND

IN considering the outlook for Great Britain, one cannot overlook the fact that while countries like the United States, with a home market of large extent practically secured to them by a high tariff wall, have opportunities for the disposal of their surpluses all over the world, this country has neither home nor foreign markets that can be absolutely relied on, except within very narrow limits. Hence the American, and to a large extent the German manufacturer, can depend upon marketing his produce within much wider limits of demand than his British compeer. Some friends of my own have only one reply to make to those who suggest lack of enterprise and apparent contentment with small yields—there is no market to rely on that would justify our producers of iron and steel in following American lines. This is no doubt true—with reservations. There is no obvious reason why, if we are to make iron at all, we should not make it under the best and most economical conditions possible to us. We could hardly lose anything if we raised the productiveness of our plants, reduced the number of hands employed for a given output of iron or steel, and got a larger annual production per unit of capital invested. British pig-iron-makers appear to be able to get only an average annual output of about 26,000 tons per furnace, while the American average is 70,000 tons, and the average of the bituminous furnaces only is over 90,000 tons. As with blast furnaces, so with

Bessemer converters and open-hearth furnaces. The American efficiency is much larger than ours.

The present capacity of the blast furnaces of the United States is about twenty-five million tons. The output of iron this year may be over twenty million tons. But when the inevitable slump comes, it may, and probably will, fall to nine or ten million tons—a figure not unknown within the last six years. Suppose that the American, with a home demand of ten million tons, produced twenty million tons of pig iron, he would have a surplus of ten million tons to send abroad. The most vulnerable market in the world of any size is our own. Hence the bulk of this quantity would probably be shipped to England. If so, is it not clear that it would entirely swamp our home markets, and cause demoralisation of prices and everything else? And this might happen quite apart from the economic conditions of the British iron industry in other respects.

GEOGRAPHICAL POSITION AND SHIPPING FACILITIES

In one respect Great Britain is, or should be, the most favoured nation in the world for carrying on a foreign trade. We have a unique command of shipping ports and of shipping resources. All other things being equal, this consideration alone should almost settle the race for commercial supremacy in our favour. While Germany has only Hamburg and Bremen, Belgium only Antwerp, France only Marseilles, Havre, Brest, and one or two others, Italy Genoa, Naples, and Palermo, among ports of the front rank, we have in this country more than fifty ports whence shipments can be made, and fifteen to twenty ports of the first importance. Even the United States, with its enormous seaboard, cannot compete with England in respect of port and harbour facilities, for on the Atlantic seaboard the only ports that can be described

as first class are New York, Baltimore, Boston, Philadelphia, Pensacola, and Galveston. Another splendid en-
dowment of British commerce is the comparatively short
distances that separate our centres of manufacture from
the sea. In the United States the chief centres of the
iron industry are, as we have seen, in the order of their
importance, Pittsburg, nearly 500 miles from the sea;
Chicago, nearly 1,000 miles; Cleveland, which is over
1,000 miles; and Philadelphia, which is not more than
100 miles from tide-water. The Quaker city, however, is
hardly an iron-trade centre in the sense in which the
other cities are; although important steelworks are
carried on at Pencoyd, Midvale, and Lukens, all within
a few miles of Philadelphia. In this country, as I need
hardly point out, there is no centre of the iron or any
other industry more than sixty to eighty miles from
a port. The district of which Birmingham is the centre
is farther than any other, but even here there is a choice
between Bristol, Gloucester, Liverpool, and London. The
natural advantages of the British Islands are altogether
exceptional. These advantages, unfortunately, are neu-
tralised by artificial conditions, such as exceptionally high
railway rates and charges, heavy port charges, and shipping rings and conferences.

EXTENT AND VALUE OF THE BRITISH HOME
MARKETS IN IRON AND MACHINERY

The iron trade of the United Kingdom, including
its collaterals of cutlery, hardware, implements and
tools, and machinery, is one of the largest businesses
carried on in the world to-day. It is only exceeded in
magnitude by the iron trade of the United States. In
1904 the total quantity of iron and steel imported, exported, and used at home, stated in terms of pig iron, was
over 10,000,000 tons for Great Britain alone. The total

aggregate value of this trade, including the iron and steel used in the same collateral industries, is computed in the statistical report of the British Iron Trade Association for that year at about £139,500,000 sterling. Great Britain both imports and exports larger quantities of iron and steel than any other country. Large imports of iron, however, she shares with other countries, so that if by such imports she suffers she does not suffer alone; if she gains thereby, she is not the only gainer. In 1901 Germany imported iron and steel to the tune of about 400,000 tons. In 1902 the United States imported a larger volume of iron and steel than the United Kingdom. The iron and steel imports of Belgium in 1902 amounted to over 400,000 tons.

When Great Britain has sent abroad iron and steel to the amount of 4,500,000 tons, a balance of 5,500,000 tons remains for home consumption. The great bulk of the remainder is consumed in shipbuilding, in general merchant iron and steel, in foundry uses, and in the manufacture of machinery, engines, and tools of all kinds.

Our home markets are usually attacked from one or other, or from all, of three sides, the more common being pig iron, blooms, and billets; the next general category being finished material, and the final category being tools and machinery of all kinds, including boilers and engines.

The invaders of our home iron market have less difficulty in finding buyers for semi-finished material, because the number of buyers is relatively much larger than that of those who want to buy other products. There may, for example, be fifty buyers of pig iron for one of sheets, hoops, plates, or wire. Similarly, as the manufacturers of all these finished articles use bars, blooms or billets, it is much less difficult to get the latter forms of material disposed of than the former. Not only that, but the invaders of our home markets have little or no difficulty in finding out who are likely buyers of the semi-finished products mentioned, while they might have a good deal of difficulty in placing contracts for the ultimate products.

When, therefore, Continental or American manufacturers contemplate a raid on British preserves, they generally begin with pig iron, blooms, or billets. They go on from that stage to rails, wire rods, wire, plates, etc. The products *par excellence* of the United States are rails, wire rods, and nails; those of Germany, billets, bars, and finished wire; those of Great Britain, tin-plates, ship plates, and galvanised sheets. Our ship plates we now mostly use at home, but it is only some five or six years since we were manufacturing ship plates largely for Germany, France, and other Continental countries.

In the years 1901, 1902, and 1903 we received into our home markets an average of well on to 2,000,000 tons of foreign-made material, much the greater part of which would certainly have been excluded by hostile tariffs from countries like France, Russia, and the United States. Could we have displaced this enormous volume of imports by a corresponding volume of home products, the commercial results would have been very different. When a nation knows that it can practically shut out foreign-made iron and steel, the aspect of its home market becomes entirely changed. It becomes worth looking to, and instead of being, as now with our own country, an uncertain quantity, its extent and value to home producers can be fixed and determined within narrow limits of error.

No doubt, it was such a home market as this, and not one like our own, which is liable to periodical invasions that threaten to swamp it entirely, and to have its price-movements regulated by the prices of surplusage thus thrown on our hands, that Mr. Carnegie had in view when

K

he eulogised the superior merits of home markets. Probably every one in this country would agree with Mr.
Carnegie if they had the same conditions, and if they
could turn to Germany and the United States for their
dumping grounds in the same way that these countries
now turn to us. In such a case we should not only be
able to avoid the disorganising and commercially ruinous
effects of the invasions we have referred to, but we should
be able to vastly increase our exports, for we should then
be able to take a turn at getting rid of our surpluses by
the expedients that are now so familiar to them.

The quantity of iron and steel available for the purposes
of the British iron industry in 1902, in terms of pig iron,
was approximately as under :—

	Tons.
Make of pig iron in United Kingdom .	8,500,000
Imports of pig iron . . .	227,338
Imports of finished iron and steel, in terms of pig iron	1,260,978
Total . . .	9,988,316

Of this total to be dealt with, the following are estimated
details to the extent of 4,659,835 tons exported in one
form or another :—

CONSUMPTION OF PIG IRON IN EXPORT TRADE IN 1902

	Tons.
Exported as pig iron . . .	1,102,835
Wholly or partly manufactured iron and steel, in terms of pig . . .	2,833,000
Exports of machinery, in terms of pig [1] .	524,000
Exports of tools and implements, hardware, telegraph wire, motors and cycles, etc., valued at ten millions, taken as . .	200,000
Total . . .	4,659,835

[1] The machinery is taken as averaging £40 per ton, and waste is taken
at 20 per cent.

The quantity of pig iron consumed for the purposes of the home trade, apart from exports, is not quite easy of estimation. We see that the total consumption of pig iron, including home make and imports, was 9,988,316 tons. Of this volume, 4,659,835 tons were exported, leaving a balance of 5,328,481 tons for home consumption. We have now to see how this balance was disposed of. According to estimates which I recently made for the British Iron Trade Association the principal items were, as nearly as can be computed, as follows :—

		Tons.
Used in shipbuilding	. . .	1,200,000
„ as general merchant iron and steel	.	1,108,000
„ for general foundry purposes	. .	1,000,000
„ as machinery for home trade	. .	700,000
„ for tin-plates used in home market	.	220,000
„ as railway material „ „	.	450,000
„ as tools, hardware, implements, etc.	.	450,000
„ for naval and military purposes, etc.	.	200,000
Total	. . .	5,328,000

These figures demonstrate that our home trade is a good deal more important than our foreign, large as that branch of our commerce is. Of course, in a number of cases the totals can be little more than mere conjecture, but the general results are believed to be near the mark.

THE SOURCES OF DEMAND FOR IRON AND STEEL

The consumption of iron and steel varies greatly in different countries. It reaches its maximum in the United States, with about 500 lb. *per capita* per annum, and it falls to only a few pounds in such countries as China, India, and Japan. But in all countries alike there is a notable tendency towards an increase of production, and even the least civilised nations are likely, in course of time, to reach a much higher level than anything hitherto attained. If we go back to the commencement of the nineteenth century, we find that the total consumption of iron throughout the world was less than a ninth part of what it is to-day. Not more than a hundred years ago the total consumption of iron by all countries was under five million tons. To-day the total consumption is over forty-five millions. It is interesting and important to ascertain how the difference has chiefly come about.

This, of course, involves a consideration of the sources of demand that have most rapidly and largely expanded in the principal civilised countries, and notably in Great Britain. And as a preliminary to this investigation it may be pointed out that while there are some sources of demand common to all countries alike, there are others that are more or less special to particular countries. Some have a larger consumption of wire, others of rails, others of structural steel, others of sheets, others of plates for shipbuilding. The descriptions that are most universally in demand are bars for ordinary blacksmithing uses, both of iron and steel; railway rails and fishplates, which are necessary to the construction of ways of communication; wire, which is needed for fencing, for nails, and for general ironmongery purposes; and foundry iron, which is applied to the production of a great variety of castings.

The principal source of home demand for steel is the shipbuilding industry, which has annually absorbed over a million tons of finished plates and angles in the last seven years. The British demand for shipbuilding material is much greater than that of any other country. The tonnage of new vessels built in British waters has during that time been more than that of all other countries put together. Our annual output is more than 1,600,000 tons, compared with less than 950,000 tons in the United States, Germany, and France combined. In addition to the home consumption, there is still a considerable export of ship plates from Great Britain, several countries, including Germany, admitting such material free of duty.

Next to ship plates, British steelworks produce a relatively greater variety of sheets than any other steel-producing country. This is partly due to its larger trade in tin-plates, and partly to the exceptional extent of its trade in the production and export of galvanised and corrugated sheets. The collective annual output of these descriptions of sheets may be taken at approximately the following figures :—

	Home demand. Tons.		Exports. Tons.		Total. Tons.
Tin-plates . .	170,000	...	300,000	...	470,000
Black plates . .	40,000	...	60,000	...	100,000
Galvanised and corrugated sheets .	200,000	...	350,000	...	550,000

Our output of tin-plates would have been nearly twice what it is to-day had the McKinley Tariff of 1890 not been enforced. Previous to that tariff being enacted the United States were buying nearly 400,000 tons a year of tin-plates from Great Britain. Since then, the United States have built up a great tin-plate industry, and have reduced their demands for British plates to less than 60,000 tons annually. The tin-plate trade of Great Britain suffered a severe blow in the loss of the American trade, but that loss has now largely been recouped by increase of demand from other sources, and in a few years more the British output is likely to be greater than it ever was.

Apart from the railway and shipbuilding requirements of the world, one of the largest and most promising fields open in the future is that of the manufacture of so-called structural iron—that is to say, of iron or steel employed in the erection of buildings of different kinds—galvanised iron, beams, girders, pillars, joists, floorings, and so on. The statistics of this branch of the iron and steel industries are not so well kept as those of some other branches. In Great Britain nearly a dozen works have within the last few years taken up the manufacture of girders in order to meet the home demands. These works have a capacity of some 250,000 tons a year, in addition to which Great Britain imports 80,000 to 90,000 tons of similar material. In the United States the advance has been even more remarkable. There the total production of structural material exceeds a million tons, which means an advance of 200 per cent. within ten years. Iron and steel are now regularly employed in the foundations and superstructure of almost all kinds of new American buildings. A new application, of which large expectations have been formed, is the construction of roadways with a view to greater durability of the road and the reduction of the power needed to move a vehicle.

In the United States steel has, of late years, been employed to a very large extent in the construction of railway rolling stock. The quantity of steel now annually employed for this purpose is computed at fully 700,000 tons a year, whereas ten years ago the output of such structural shapes was almost trifling. There is every reason to suppose that this American example will be followed more largely in European countries, including Great Britain. Hitherto not more than 5 per cent. of the rolling stock of Great Britain has been entirely built of steel, although steel frames are becoming more general year by year. A walk along the principal thoroughfares of London and other important cities will show that steel is employed for building purposes to an infinitely greater extent than it was a few years ago, and this use appears destined to advance very greatly, and perhaps more so than any other.

The Pressed Steel Car Company built in 1902 an average of 100 steel cars per day for 300 days. In each of these cars were about 12 tons of plates and small shapes, such as angles and channels, giving a total supply of about 360,000 tons of plates by one concern in a year, and in an industry that a few years ago was practically unknown. The Standard Steel Car Company, at Butler, completed their works in August of 1902, and within a few months was making 50 steel cars per day, requiring 600 tons daily of plates and shapes. The output of the American Car and Foundry Company is about the same as that of the Standard Company. The orders for steel cars recently booked by these concerns mean that, operating to their full capacity all through the year, their combined consumption of plates would be 2,400 tons per day, or 720,000 tons per annum.

There is likely to be some diversity of opinion on the question whether the present demand for new shipbuilding, which may be put at 2½ million tons a year, is likely to be maintained, or whether the nations of the world are not overbuilding, and threatened in consequence with a glut of shipping. There is no rule-of-three proposition whereby this problem may be solved. But it is a matter of the most common knowledge that in a hundred different directions the carrying trade of the world has been increasing of late years, and is likely to continue to increase. Take two items only as an evidence of this development. Within the last twenty years the exports of coal from different countries, including Great Britain, have considerably more than doubled, and now represent an aggregate of over seventy million tons a year. Within the same period the quantity of iron ore carried oversea to and from different countries has advanced from less than three million to thirteen million tons, and it is likely to reach a much higher figure.

Then, again, there has been an enormously increased demand for iron and steel in consequence of the great extent to which steam tonnage has displaced, and is still displacing, sailing tonnage. In the five years ending 1892 about 24 per cent. of all the new tonnage built in the United Kingdom was constructed for wind propulsion, whereas in the five years ending 1902, less than 8 per cent. of the total new tonnage was constructed to make use of wind. This change is a very marked and important one, and involves a much larger employment of iron and steel in the construction of marine engines, boilers, pumps, and other mechanical accessories employed on the average steamship. There can be little doubt that this is likely to be a permanent movement, and that the days of sailing tonnage for purely mercantile purposes, are practically over, except in certain out-of-the-way localities, where freight rates are probably of less importance than in the great ocean highways.

The demands for railway iron and steel are constantly increasing, and are likely to continue to do so. Previous to 1825, when the first passenger railway—the Stockton and Darlington—was opened, such demands were almost *nil*. To-day the annual output of railway rails, chairs, sleepers, bolts, and fishplates exceeds six million tons, so far as can be ascertained. The demand would have been at least three times that figure had not the Bessemer process provided a material that has a life equal to the extent of that difference, compared with malleable iron rails, the material which it has now, for railway purposes, almost universally displaced. The rail trade of Great Britain has not made much progress in foreign countries for nearly twenty years past, mainly because British exports to the United States and to other countries that now largely or wholly supply themselves have fallen off; but the average rail exports of British works are still larger than those of any other country.

The manufacture of tubes is a branch of the steel trade

MOTOR DRIVEN ARMOUR PLATE ROLLS

that has within recent years assumed very large dimensions. There are no exact records of the output of British tubes, but it is approximately computed at over 450,000 tons annually. The requirements of hydraulic mining, of oil-pipe lines, and of telegraph, telephone, and other electrical purposes, have created a constantly increasing demand for tubes, which is likely to go to a much greater length than hitherto.

We might pursue this inquiry into the fields occupied by the more minute applications of iron and steel, but that seems to be unnecessary, as the only object of this section is to indicate the extent and the character of the demand for the leading products by way of helping a computation as to the prospects of the future. The outlook cannot be more suitably indicated than by a reference to the fact that in the last twelve years the output of steel throughout the world has almost doubled, while within the last twenty years the world's make of pig iron has more than doubled. If the future should witness as great a development of iron and steel wants as the immediate past has done, there need be no fear that those who have iron and steel to dispose of at reasonable prices will not be able to dispose of them, however much there may be flux and reflux in the incidents and movements of general demand.

CHAPTER XIV

BRITISH COLONIAL MARKETS

I T would be natural to assume that a country which possesses the enormous variety and extent of colonial dominions that own the sway of the British crown should have all the advantage of the old-fashioned and now more or less discredited aphorism that " trade follows the flag." The experience of both the mother country and her colonies for many years past has shown that trade has a perverse habit of following the lowest prices, irrespective of flag, and this has encouraged rival nations to enter into a keen competition for the business in iron and steel of the British colonies in every part of the world.

CANADA

The largest individual market among the British colonies is Canada. This Dominion imports something approaching a million tons of iron and steel annually, and is likely to considerably increase this volume within the next few years. The output of iron and steel in Canada is also growing. The make of pig iron has increased from less than 50,000 tons to more than 350,000 within the last decade. The output of steel is not yet 250,000 tons a year. Considerable establishments have, however, been built in Nova Scotia (Cape Breton more especially), Ontario, and Quebec for producing both iron and steel, and all arrangements have been made to ensure a much greater home industry than that hitherto established.

The special case of the Dominion illustrates with great

emphasis the influence of proximity of geographical position and of a tariff system in developing a foreign trade. Twenty-five years ago, Great Britain supplied the bulk of the iron and steel requirements of Canada— the United States only contributing 20 to 30 per cent. against 70 to 80 per cent. supplied by the mother country. But for the last ten years, the United States have provided 70 to 80 per cent., while the mother land has only supplied 20 to 30 per cent.

The total values of the Canadian imports and exports of iron and steel for the last five years compare as under —in thousands of dollars:—

Year.	Value of Imports.	Value of Exports.
1899	. . . 19,848	... 2,817
1900	. . . 26,649	... 3,462
1901	. . . 27,107	... 3,717
1902	. . . 33,681	... 6,027
1903	. . . 42,156	... 6,849

These figures include cutlery, hardware, and machinery. They make it clear that the value of our colonial trade may within a very few years assume much greater proportions, seeing that within the last five years Canada's has more than doubled.

The average *ad val.* rate of duty paid on dutiable imports from Great Britain was 23·3 per cent. in 1903, against 24·9 per cent. paid on dutiable imports from the United States. The average *ad val.* rate on both free and dutiable goods for the same year was 16·7 per cent. in the case of Great Britain and 13·2 per cent. in the case of the United States.

In 1903, 57·2 per cent. of the total imports of Canada were received from the United States and 26·1 per cent. from Great Britain. In the previous year the corresponding percentages were 24·9 and 58·4 per cent.

To make the influence of the Canadian tariff understood, as affecting iron and steel imports, the following statement showing the values of the receipts of iron and steel under the two heads of dutiable and non-dutiable is submitted :—

IMPORTS OF IRON, STEEL, ETC., INTO CANADA IN
THOUSANDS OF DOLLARS

1903.	From United States.		United Kingdom.		Other Countries.		Total.
Dutiable	. 12,406	...	7,029	...	2,346	...	21,781
Free .	. 5,433	...	2,777	...	1,279	...	9,489
1902.							
Dutiable	. 11,016	...	4,399	...	763	...	31,270
Free .	. 5,036	...	1,597	...	2,238	...	8,871
1901.							
Dutiable	. 10,273	...	2,049	...	380	...	24,288
Free .	. 5,524	...	753	...	139	...	12,219

VALUES OF IMPORTS OF IRON, STEEL, AND MACHINERY
INTO CANADA FROM UNITED STATES AND
UNITED KINGDOM

Year.	Iron and Steel.		Machinery.		Implements.	
	U.S.	U.K.	U.S.	U.K.	U.S.	U.K.
1901 .	15,798	2,802	5,451	579	1,862	22
1902 .	16,053	5,996	5,906	379	2,635	20
1903 .	17,840	9,806	7,462	322	3,147	23
Total	49,691	18,604	18,819	1,280	7,644	65

These figures show that in all three categories the imports from the United States for the three years were 76,153,000 dollars, compared with 20,949,000 dollars imported from Great Britain, so that the difference was 55,204,000 dollars, or 263 per cent. against the old country.

Although the iron industry has been carried on in Canada for more than a hundred years, it has never hitherto been followed on a scale of great importance. Until within the last ten years, the output of pig iron has not, in any one year, reached 60,000 tons a year. The business has mainly been carried on in the provinces of Quebec and Ontario, which are almost without mineral fuel, and hence it has been necessary to use charcoal instead of coke for smelting. This has both limited the output and rendered the iron a relatively dear product.

The earlier Canadian attempts to produce iron and steel have not been entirely successful. Some of them may be spoken of as disastrous. In this category is the enterprise of the Steel Company of Canada, at London-derry, Nova Scotia, which was started in 1873, with a capital of 2,500,000 dollars, to purchase the Acadian Iron Mines there, and undertake the manufacture of steel rails, etc., on a large scale by the open-hearth process. In this enterprise the late Sir William Siemens was engaged. The company erected two large blast furnaces, and several melting furnaces and rotators to carry on the Siemens direct process. They manufactured castings, car wheels, rolls, ships' knees, and other products of a more or less special character, but as the home demand was very limited, and there was not much scope for an export business, the concern had ultimately to be wound up.

No further attempts were made in the Dominion to produce steel on a scale of importance until in 1899 the Dominion Iron and Steel Company, promoted by Mr. Whitney, of Boston, was launched at Sydney, Cape Breton, to smelt pig iron, and produce therefrom rails, billets, plates, and other descriptions of steel, using New-foundland iron ores and local coal and coke. This company has, since its inception, had as chequered a career as the Steel Company of Canada, but it seems to be built on more sound foundations than was that ill-starred enter-prise. It has four blast furnaces, each capable of pro-ducing nearly 2,000 tons of pig iron per week, ten open-hearth furnaces of nearly forty tons capacity each, and three rolling mills. Cheap pig iron can undoubtedly be made at Sydney, the coke being on the spot, and the ore being delivered alongside blast furnaces, at less than two dollars per ton (48 to 50 per cent.). The utmost that this iron should cost to produce is 40s. per ton, and as there is a bounty of two dollars per ton, paid by the Government, the net cost of the product on tide-water is probably not more than 30s. per ton.

Other recent Canadian iron and steel works have been established at North Sydney, Cape Breton; at the Soo Ste. Marie, in Ontario, and at Collingwood, on Lake Huron. These works, and those of the Dominion Company, have collectively a capacity to produce nearly a million tons of pig iron and probably 650,000 tons of steel annually; but the actual output, for various reasons, has never approached those figures. One of these reasons is that the principal works, situated in Nova Scotia, are a long distance from the chief centres of consumption, and the same remark applies to the "Soo" works in Ontario. At any rate, the greatest quantity of pig iron hitherto produced in Canada in any one year has been rather over 350,000 tons, including charcoal iron, while the utmost output of steel has been under 150,000 tons. As the annual consumption of the Dominion is about a million tons, the bulk of the demand is met by imports, of which about 70 per cent. is contributed by the United States, and rather over 30 per cent. by Great Britain and other countries.

The ironmaking resources of Canada are not of the best, but they should be equal to building up, in course of time, a very considerable industry. Iron ores are found in every one of the provinces of the Dominion, but probably most largely, and of the best quality, in Vancouver. Nova Scotia has iron ores scattered over a wide area, and they have been pretty fully located, explored, and described by

Dawson and others; but few, if any, of the deposits can be regarded as of the first importance, and certainly none of them, so far proved, approach in magnitude and value the Lake Superior deposits of the United States, or even the extensive deposits worked in the neighbourhood of Birmingham, Alabama. Ontario possesses large iron ore deposits, some of them near to the Lake Superior ores on the other side of the Line, but they have not so far been found to be of great value, and in the absence of coal they are expensive to work. The North-West Territories and Vancouver are too remote, and the population is too meagre, to raise any reasonable hopes of a successful iron industry for many years to come. The principal hope of Canada, therefore, appears to rest on the development of the iron industry of the maritime provinces, and more especially of that of Nova Scotia, whence an export trade has already been done, both in iron and in steel, that may, in course of time, assume more considerable dimensions.

AUSTRALASIA

Next to Canada, the greatest buyer of British iron and steel among the colonies is Australasia. The total volume of British exports of those metals to this continent over the last five years, has fluctuated between 400,000 tons and 500,000 tons. It would have been materially greater but for the competition of Germany, Belgium, and the United States. These three countries unitedly send to the Australasian colonies well on to eighty thousand tons annually of those products. Germany is the leading source of supply of these three nations. The Australasian colonies practically depend entirely on imports. No works exist in the colonies for the manufacture of pig iron, or of steel, on a scale worth speaking of, although there are two or three small open-hearth furnaces in use for meeting very local needs. Several attempts have been made to establish ironworks in one or other of the Australasian colonies, but hitherto none have been successful on a large scale.

The Australasian colonies are richly endowed with the necessary raw materials for the prosecution of a successful iron industry on a large scale, but they have not as yet, and are hardly likely in the near future to possess, a sufficient population to support such a business. Several attempts have already been made at different times to found an Australasian iron industry—in Victoria, in New South Wales, in New Zealand, and in Queensland ; but all such attempts, with one exception, have been unsuccessful, and that exception is not of great importance.

This result is not due to the want of a considerable demand for iron and steel products. On the contrary, that demand is very important, and is growing from day to day. It is met, not by Great Britain alone, but by Germany, Belgium, and the United States as well, so that the Australian consumer has a large and sufficient choice of producers. The population of the Commonwealth is not yet much over three millions ; but three millions of people, at the American average of 500 lb. *per capita* per year, can provide a market for 700,000 tons of material annually ; and there is no reason to suppose that the Australasian average is likely long to remain much under that of the United States. On the contrary, the *per capita* consumption of iron is a function of extent of territory as well as of population ; and the territory of the Australasian colonies in relation to population can hardly be equalled elsewhere.

Of the several colonies on the Australasian continent, New South Wales and New Zealand appear to offer the best inducements for undertaking an iron industry, both because they have large iron ore supplies, and because their coal is ample, satisfactory, and not too distant from either iron ores or the seaboard.

The Department of Mines has in both colonies had important, if not also exhaustive, surveys made of the mineral resources already located, and a recent Report of the Department for New South Wales declared that they " hoped before long to be in a position to assist those who contemplate the erection of works for the smelting of the colonial ores, and finally establishing an iron industry in the colony." I have, in the course of my connection with the iron trade of Great Britain, been frequently consulted as to the outlook for manufacturing in Australia, but quite recently I have had put before me the details of an enterprise, of which my friend Mr. Enoch James, of Cardiff, is the technical adviser, that looks more promising than any other.

At the present time the Eskbank Ironworks, at Lithgow, is the only enterprise of its kind in this colony ; they produce from 6,500 to 8,000 tons annually of finished iron. From 10,000 to 12,000 tons of iron ore are raised annually as a flux for metallurgical furnaces.

SOUTH AFRICA

The great variety of the resources of South Africa, its enormous territory, its splendid climate, its admirable coal-beds, and its considerable iron ore deposits, all lead to the anticipation of an ultimate iron industry ; but that event must be preceded by an increase of the existing population, and by an extension of the means of communication. Coal is already being worked to a material extent in Natal and in the Transvaal. Its existence has been proved in other parts of the country subject to British rule, and there is no reason to doubt that by-and-by the demand for iron products will be greatly increased.

L

Indeed, it is reported that already a blast furnace has been built to smelt iron ores worked in the neighbourhood of Pretoria, and that Natal is bent on the same end.

INDIA

India has a remarkably limited import trade in iron and steel for a country of such vast extent and population, but hitherto iron has been very little required on a large scale, except for railway purposes, and so far as small local needs are concerned, these are still, to some extent, supplied by the natives, through the medium of their old-fashioned, primitive forges. The annual volume of iron and steel imports into India has within the last ten years ranged from a maximum of 650,000 tons to a minimum of 400,000 tons. There is no country making any pretensions to civilisation with so small a consumption of iron *per capita*. Pig iron is made to the extent of about 50,000 tons a year, by the Bengal Iron Company, at Barrakur, but otherwise no pig iron is made in the Empire by modern processes. A new steel-manufacturing plant has recently been built by this company adjacent to its blast furnaces.

Our great Indian Empire can hardly be said to possess an iron industry, except such as has been worked on primitive lines for hundreds of years. Various attempts have been made to establish a modern iron industry in Madras, in Calcutta, and in Bengal. It may practically be said that they have all failed, except one—the enterprise carried on for a number of years past, near Warora, by the Bengal Iron and Steel Company, which, after having produced pig iron only for a number of years, has now undertaken to add a steel plant to its establishment. Perhaps four-fifths of the total iron and steel consumed in India is still imported from Great Britain, Germany, and Belgium, in the form of wrought iron and steel. The total imports into the country are well on to a million tons a year.

The latest reports on the subject state that in Bengal and the Central Provinces the conditions of the iron industry are not encouraging. The production of ore and the manufacture of iron are declining before the competition of European iron, and in most districts the comparatively few persons engaged in the trade obtain only a bare subsistence. Primitive methods of mining and smelting, and lack of capital, are the chief drawbacks. The iron is generally of good quality, but the European metal is imported in forms much easier to work than the native make, while in many instances English-made implements are preferred because they are cheaper and have a better finish than the Indian-manufactured articles. These remarks are specially applicable to the Central Provinces. The great need is a market for the iron, and until this is found the efforts of the Forest Department to assist iron smelters by cheapening fuel and reducing royalties are not of much avail. It has been recognised that the native charcoal iron cannot compete with the ordinary kinds of iron and steel made with mineral coal, which are being imported and sold at low rates. Attempts are being made, therefore, to create a demand for the native iron similar to that which exists in Europe for Swedish charcoal pig, which sells at from 80s. to 100s. a ton. It is stated that if the railways could utilise the local iron the industry would rise at once. The only other hope for the business lies in increasing the output and reducing the cost of production, so as to enable the home product to compete with the imported article; but to effectually place the native manufacture on a level with its competitor, the introduction of modern rolling machinery is necessary.

The iron-producing districts of the Central Provinces

are Sagar, Jabalpur, Mandla, Seoni, Narsinghpur, Chanda, Bhandara, Balaghat, Raipur, and Sambalpur. In every case the production is very small, and the processes employed are of the most primitive kind.

The native iron furnaces in Mandla are worked on annual licences, issued by the Forest Department, eight rupees a year being charged for a single furnace, twelve rupees for two, and fifteen rupees for the use of three furnaces. The licence fee includes the royalty, estimated at four rupees per furnace, and the cost of fuel and charcoal used by the smelters. The quarrying cost amounts to three rupees. The annual earnings of the smelters are from twenty-five rupees to thirty rupees per furnace. The working cost is much greater in Raipur, where the net profit is considerably more. In return for a royalty of eleven rupees per furnace, paid to the zemindar, the workers use as much ore as they can throughout the year. They have, however, to expend nearly Rs. 400 per furnace per year for quarrying and charcoal. Thus the total yearly cost for each furnace is Rs. 411. The gross receipts on the year's work amount to Rs. 600, and the net profit is nearly Rs. 189. To obtain this result 9,600 seers of iron ore have to be smelted by each furnace, the smelted iron being sold at the rate of four seers per rupee. About four seers of ore are required to produce one seer of the smelted metal.

There is every reason to believe that India will, by-and-by, become a much larger consumer of iron and steel. Except the Chinese Empire, the present *per capita* consumption of India is less than that of any other civilised country. The imports of British iron and steel have of late materially increased, and they now exceed half a million tons annually. India is wedded to old methods and traditions, and hence the consumption of malleable iron is relatively greater than in any other country. No modern steelworks of any importance have hitherto been established. Both Germany and Belgium compete for the Indian market with some success. Their united iron exports to India are about one-fifth of those of Great Britain.

OTHER BRITISH COLONIES

Although in Canada, Australasia, South Africa, and India Britain finds her chief colonial markets, and the markets from which the greatest things are hoped for in the future, there are numerous other British Colonies, of smaller extent, whose demands in the aggregate have of late years shown a considerable increase, and are likely to continue to increase in the future. Newfoundland, Ceylon, the West Indies, the Straits Settlements, and Fiji are among the more notable of these. It is not necessary to give details of trade in each case.

CHAPTER XV

GREAT BRITAIN'S FOREIGN TRADE IN IRON AND STEEL

DURING the twenty years ended with 1880, Great Britain rapidly built up a very large and important trade in the exportation of her iron and steel manufactures. That business culminated in a total export of 4,353,000 tons in 1882. This volume has never since been equalled, so that it remains our record after an interval of more than twenty-three years.

In the earlier years of the same century our exports were very trifling, and their growth was slow. In the year 1820 we sent abroad 91,763 tons of all sorts, of which bar iron constituted more than one-half, and pig iron (which is now, and has for many years past been, the largest individual item of export) was only 5,631 tons, or about one-eighth of our bar-iron exports. It should be added that the total exports of 1820, given above, included 6,697 tons of hardware and cutlery, which have long been removed from the general category of our iron and steel exports, and of which the volume has not for many years been ascertainable. It also included 7,937 tons of bolt and rod iron, which is so nearly akin to bar iron that the two may be regarded as almost one. Taking these two factors into account, the bar iron exports of 1820 were 64 per cent. of our total iron and steel exports of all kinds. It may be added that

AMERICAN BILLET MILL.

the average declared value of this iron was over £9 per ton.

A number of extremely important categories, since filling leading places in our export returns, were entirely absent from the shipments of the year 1890. The most important of these items were railway material, tin-plates, black plates for tinning, and galvanised and corrugated sheets. Steel was not exported in any form, except as cutlery or hardware.

In the record year of maximum exports—1882—our greatest individual export was pig iron, of which the total shipment was 1,758,000 tons. This figure fell three years later to 961,000 tons, and has never in any subsequent year been equalled.

The next most important individual item was railroad iron, of which the shipments exceeded 971,000 tons. This figure has been equalled, but rarely exceeded. The third item that calls for comment is bar, angle and rod iron, of which we shipped over 313,000 tons, and this figure again is one that has not since been equalled. In the volume of our exports of sheets and plates, wire, and other descriptions, the variations have not, in the interval, been so notable as in the cases just mentioned.

The main difference between 1882 and more recent years has been that we had then the United States as a practically open market, whereas for the last ten or twelve years, excepting for 1902 and 1903, it has practically been shut upon us. There is a not uncommon impression that our iron exports are generally declining, but this is not the case. If we deduct American imports from our total shipments in 1882, the result is that we have a considerably smaller remainder than the average annual volume of our exports over the last ten years. In the four years ended with 1882 we shipped about four and a half million tons of iron and steel to the United States alone. If we deduct these shipments from our total exports, we find that our American trade is almost alone responsible for what is now the difference in our total iron and steel shipments, compared with earlier periods. It is necessary to keep these facts in mind in considering the conditions and fluctuations, as well as the general movement, of our export business.

During the last five years our imports of iron and steel have considerably more than doubled. The increase has mainly been made up of unworked steel—blooms, billets, and bars.

In 1860 our total iron and steel imports were 56,683 tons; in 1870 they rose to 102,069 tons; in 1880 they were 275,407 tons; in 1890, 323,840 tons; and in 1903, 1,299,000 tons. The movement was a more or less steadily progressive one, which culminated in 1903 in the greatest volume of iron and steel imports on record.

In the earlier history of the trade relatively large quantities of iron and steel were imported from Russia, Sweden, France, and Spain, and in some years our imports exceeded our exports. In 1903 our exports of iron and steel were about three times the volume of our imports, and more than three times their value. In 1900 our exports were twelve times the volume and seven times the value of our imports. During the last few years there has been a notable change in the character and conditions of our iron and steel import trade. In former years it was less strictly competitive than it has now become. Up to about 1885 our principal import consisted of Swedish bar iron, which was designed for use in our crucible-steel industry, and was, in effect, a high-class and special raw material, which was not produced of kindred quality in Great Britain, and was non-competitive. Since then, the imports of bar iron of this character have relatively much declined, and the business is now chiefly made up of products that are in every sense competitive, such as blooms and billets, general merchant and structural steel, steel rails and plates, and other descriptions which are sent into our markets, not because we cannot produce them equally well, but because it suits the nations concerned to export them into a market that is open to all and sundry, without let or hindrance.

Up to the year 1885 we imported a considerably smaller quantity of iron and steel than the United States, Germany, France, or Belgium. To-day we import larger quantities of iron and steel than any other nation, and our normal imports may be regarded as three times those of any country in Europe.

Until a comparatively recent date no other country exported iron and steel on a scale comparable with that of our own exports. Sweden was the only other country that exported iron and steel on a scale of any importance thirty years ago. It is true that German and Belgian competition was not then entirely unknown, but it was far from being the serious and enormous business that it has since become. The United States did not begin to export on a scale of any magnitude until 1896, and no other country has yet taken a position of any real importance in this international competition. Practically the foreign markets of the world are now supplied by three countries —Great Britain, Germany, and the United States.

The following figures show the destinations of the total exports of these three countries in thousands of tons :—

	1898.	1902.	Increase or Decrease in four years.
The United States, Great Britain, and Germany	1,202=20%	2,100=29%	+74%
Other European markets	2,380=40%	2,160=30%	− 9%
Countries outside of Europe, excluding U.S.	2,336=40%	2,916=40%	− 20%
Total exports of all three countries	5,918=100	7,176=100	+21%

The movement of the export trade of the three leading countries during the six years ended 1903 is set out in the next statement.

IRON AND STEEL EXPORTS AND IMPORTS IN THOUSANDS OF METRICAL TONS

Year.			UNITED STATES.		GERMANY.		GREAT BRITAIN.	
			Exports.	Imports.	Exports.	Imports.	Exports.	Imports.
1897	.	.	561	162	1,069	524	3,318	—
1898	.	.	797	146	1,279	483	2,902	591
1899	.	.	894	175	1,129	778	3,368	645
1900	.	.	1·123	210	1,155	923	3,213	761
1901	.	.	668	221	1,917	358	2,617	869
1902	.	.	332	1,212	2,832	234	3,241	1,041
First half, 1903		.	137	780	1,570	113	1,743	630
Second ,, ,,		.	135	400	1,370	164	1,466	691

The general result brought out by these figures manifestly is that the export trade of the world in iron and steel is rapidly being developed, but one of the remarkable features of this development is that countries which are themselves largely engaged in the exportation of iron and steel are also important importers of these metals. A large part of the increased exports of iron within late years has been sent to Great Britain by Germany and the United States. A smaller, but still very considerable part of the increase is that of iron and steel sent into Belgium by Germany. The British Colonies are becoming much larger importers, and Germany, Belgium, and the United States are taking a large slice of this increased demand.

The export trade in iron and steel is in all countries liable to remarkable fluctuations. The recent statistical history of the United States shows this very clearly. The imports into that country in 1902–3 were three times the average of the five previous years, while the exports fell to less than one-half of what they had been in 1899–1900. It has been the same in Germany and in our own country. Within four years the volume of British exports has fluctuated by over 1,000,000 tons. In the case of the German iron trade, the exports of 1903, which were within 8 per cent. of those of Great Britain for the same year, had doubled within eight years. Such cases point to the great uncertainty, under existing conditions, of both the import and the export trade.

These remarks apply to the general volume of foreign trade. There are particular cases in which they are not so applicable. One such case is that of the imports into this country of Swedish bar iron, which for certain purposes has not yet been displaced. Another such case is that of our exports of tin-plates to the United States up to the passing of the McKinley Tariff in 1890. In both these cases the business done had much of the character of a monopoly. Here, however, their identity ceases. The Swedish bar trade has been reduced by the substitution of open-hearth steel of high quality produced at home. The Welsh tin-plate exports to the United States have been reduced from a maximum of 448,000 tons a year to a minimum of about 50,000 tons by the building up of a rival industry on American soil. The case of the imports of pig iron into Germany differs from both. In each of the years 1899 and 1900, the Germans imported, mainly from this country, about 660,000 tons of pig iron, which in 1901 was reduced to 267,503 tons, and has since been further diminished, owing to the increased resources of production created in Germany herself, but not as a result of increased protection.

The history of the iron trade proves that much may be done to consolidate an export trade by giving special attention to the conditions required for the cultivation of individual products. As a matter of fact, each country that has a considerable export trade has been largely aided by attention to this point. The principal features of the export iron trade of Great Britain are pig iron, plates, and sheets. Those of Germany are blooms and billets, structural steel, and wire. Those of the United States, in so far as they can be estimated, are rails, wire nails, and one or two other descriptions.

It is one of the statistical curiosities of the American iron trade—and a phenomenon not at all unknown in the iron trade of other countries—that large imports coincide with large exports of the same products. Thus, while the Americans imported in 1902–3 22,990 tons of wire rods, they also exported 31,857 tons of the same commodity, due, no doubt, to price considerations. There is, however, one item of trade in which the Americans have not as yet succeeded in making much headway. They only exported 694 tons of tin-plates in 1903, and 1,074 tons in the previous year. Against this they imported 88,838 tons in 1902, and reduced that figure to 49,068 tons in 1903, so that, if they have not displaced British tin-plates in foreign markets, they continue to do so in their own.

The only other item that appears to call for remark in the iron and steel imports of the United States is that of old iron and steel. This was 135,901 tons in 1903, against only 49,188 tons in the previous year. In so far as these quantities were furnished by Great Britain, it is probably not a matter for regret that they are likely to be reduced, since our home supplies of old metal available for the open-hearth process are none too abundant, and may before long become really scarce.

The following figures show at a glance how the imports

and exports of iron and steel compare with their production in 1904 in the principal countries :—

	PIG-IRON Production. 1 = 1,000 metrical tons.	Percentage of Home Production. Imported. Per cent.	Exported. Per cent.
Great Britain . . .	8,562	2·5 ...	10·8
Germany . . .	10,104	3·4 ...	1·9
France . . .	3,000	2·9 ...	5·2
Belgium . . .	1,283	16·2 ...	1·6
Austria-Hungary . .	1,408	4·6 ...	1·5
United States . .	16,497	0·4 ...	0·5

FINISHED IRON AND STEEL

Great Britain . . .	5,500	12·7 ...	35·3
Germany . . .	9,695	1·4 ...	25·0
France . . .	2,037	3·5 ...	8·0
Belgium . . .	1,430	10·4 ...	30·1
Austria-Hungary . .	1,034	3·6 ...	7·3
United States . .	12,013	2·2 ...	4·2

The following figures show the growth of British exports of steam engines and other machinery :—

Year.		Annual value. £		Increase of value. £
1840	...	593,065	...	———
1850	...	1,042,166	...	449,101
1860	...	3,837,821	...	1,795,655
1870	...	5,293,273	...	1,455,452
Average of 1878–82	...	9,186,627	...	3,893,354
„ 1888–92	...	14,864,542	...	5,677,915
„ 1898–1902	...	18,662,430	...	3,797,888
1904	...	21,082,502	...	2,420,072

These two tables should be instructive as illustrating the comparative conditions of output and foreign trade in the six leading iron-producing countries, and the rapid and remarkable expansion of the great mechanical industries of our own country.

CHAPTER XVI

DUMPING CONDITIONS AND INTERNATIONAL COMPETITION

DUMPING IN THEORY AND IN PRACTICE

THE last two years have coincided with a remarkable agitation in Great Britain directed against the importation into the country of foreign supplies of iron and steel, which are sold at less than the prices current in British markets. This system, which has assumed large dimensions, is described as "dumping." The principal dumping nations have been Germany, the United States, and Belgium. Germany has been more conspicuous and persistent in this direction than any other country. The United States have dumped more or less intermittently, and it has been a question whether Belgium could be reckoned among the dumping nations at all.

While the manufacturers of the United States have been by no means such determined dumpers in times past as the Germans, they are more or less influenced by the same circumstances, and especially by the fact that their output of both iron and steel has now reached dimensions far in excess of anything like normal home demands, plus the possible legitimate needs of suitable markets. The ordinary home demands of a country are mainly a function of population. The United States have to-day a population of 80,000,000 of people, Germany has 56,000,000, and Great Britain has 42,000,000. Until quite lately Great Britain had the greatest *per capita* consumption of iron and steel. To-day that enviable distinction belongs to the United States, which in 1904 had an average *per capita* consumption of about 500 lb. —a larger figure than was ever attained in Great Britain. Germany, which in 1903 had produced about 10,200,000 tons of pig iron, has an annual home consumption of about 7,000,000 tons, in terms of pig, which represents an average of about 300 lb. per head.

The most marvellous feature of the American iron industry is the great advance of *per capita* consumption during recent years. In the year 1890, when the United States for the first time produced over nine million tons of pig iron, enabling her to take the lead of Great Britain as an iron producer, her *per capita* consumption was only about 300 lb. per head, so that in the interval there has been an increased consumption per head of 200 lb., or about 70 per cent.

In this comparison, however, two exceptionally good years are compared. The average of the previous and intervening years was much less than the figures of either 1890 or 1904. An average of the whole period would be under 400 lb. *per capita*. Hence it is clear that the consumption of iron is an uncertain quantity, and may either fully tax the productive resources of the country or fall very far below them. It is this uncertainty that exposes the chief industrial nations to the constant danger of having their home market falling short of the provision made for meeting its demands, and compels a search for foreign markets, which, in the last resort, can only be satisfied by a process of dumping.

The United States must always be placed at a disadvantage by the great distances that separate their principal industrial centres from the sea. They have also to contend with the necessity for paying a higher range of wages than that paid in any competitive country, whereby the cost of production, *ceteris paribus*, is, of course, made relatively higher. They have, finally, to fight against a climate which, while delightful over a large part of the year, is usually over a great range of its area exceptionally hot in summer and extremely cold in winter, so that continuous labour under high pressure is less easily maintained than it would be under less extreme climatic conditions.

All this makes the necessities and the facilities of the United States more or less difficult to reconcile. It is true that in the past no nation has won greater triumphs in the international field. But there is a widespread and increasing belief that those achievements were to a large extent founded on bluff, and carried out under conditions that cannot easily be repeated. It is commonly believed, for example—even in America—that the low prices of minerals, iron, and steel, that prevailed over the period 1893-7 are not likely to be repeated, and could hardly under normal circumstances be repeated, without heavy loss. Whether this view is realised in actual experience time alone can tell. It is not put forward here as entirely free from liability to error, but it has at least the colour of probability. If it should prove to be correct, then it would seem to follow that the entrance of the United States upon the stage of foreign markets is likely to be made, and its place there maintained, not through the flowery meads of satisfactory profits, but by the side-door that leads to the dump-heap.

The dumping of American iron and steel into Great Britain may be regarded as having had a beginning in the year 1896. Up to that year the total annual value of the imports of those products from the United States did not exceed £600,000 in any one year. But in 1896 the value was £1,591,000; in 1897 it rose to £2,422,000; and in 1899 it was £3,808,000. Here there was a more than five-

fold increase within five years. At the same time, this
increase was not entirely due to what are usually regarded
as dumping conditions, for in the years 1899 and 1900 the
British manufacturers had so much work on hand that
they had the utmost difficulty in meeting the demands
of customers, and they were therefore in many cases glad
to make purchases from the United States at almost any
price. Since 1899 our imports of American iron and steel
had materially fallen off until 1904.

Of the £100,000,000 sterling which we now expend
annually on the manufactured products of other countries,
nearly twenty millions go for iron, steel, and manufactured
goods in those metals, such as cycles, motors, sewing
machines, and machinery generally. Unquestionably,
therefore, those industries have a special claim to be heard
on this subject. No other industry is so much affected by
large importations of foreign manufactures. There is
some difficulty in deciding as to the how and the wherefore
of this notable fact. Why should the iron and machinery
trades be specially subject to invasion? Why not equally
textile industries, chemical industries, and other staples?
Every one of these has its turn, no doubt, and if un-
restricted invasion of our markets is continued, the end
of it will be as serious for some others as it threatens
to be for iron and machinery.

No better illustration of the conditions under which
dumping is carried on could perhaps be afforded than
that furnished by the experience of the wire industry. In
a recent six months the German Wire Rod Syndicate,
which comprises eighty-two works, sold 41,831 tons of
wire rods. Of this quantity 22,307 tons were disposed
of in Germany, whilst the remaining 19,524 tons were
sold abroad. The profit realised from the inland sales
amounted to £58,856, whereas, in the case of the exports,
which were only 2,783 tons less than the quantity con-

M

sumed in Germany, there was a loss of £42,972. The explanation of the difference is afforded by the fact that German consumers were compelled to pay for the privilege of enabling the syndicate to conduct an export trade, they having been charged £12 10s. a ton, as against £7 per ton charged for the exported goods.

The agitation that has been carried on against dumping in Great Britain for some time has, however, been partly founded on a more or less imperfect ascertainment of essential facts. A correspondent recently sent me a list of twenty-nine ironworks in South Wales which were alleged to have been closed by dumping, and requested me to give the true facts of each case. These, shortly, were that four-fifths of the works on the list were either old finished-iron works, or obsolete tin-plate works, and in both cases dumping had nothing to do with their becoming derelict. South Wales, thirty years ago, produced well on to a million tons of finished iron annually. To-day the output is not 20,000 tons. The place of finished iron has been taken by steel, and the revolution has necessarily led to a number of the old works being closed. In the case of other works, they were unfavourably situated, or had been allowed to get so far behind the standard of present-day efficiency that they could only have been profitably worked under extraordinary conditions. That the rank and file of the trade had a certain confidence in the future is proved by the fact that within the last fifteen years about twenty-six steelworks have been built in this district, whose capacity for producing steel to-day is twice as great as its greatest capacity for the production of finished iron in the past.

The question has been discussed whether Great Britain or any other country similarly situated, that receives dumped material, does not, on the whole, gain more than is lost by the process. This is a complex question, but it is so important as to demand serious consideration.

The influence, be it observed, is not limited to our own home markets. The Canadian market may be cited as one that has been seriously affected and largely lost to British producers, by the dumping of the United States. The influence is widespread and insidious, and applies more or less to all outside markets. We have seen that in Canada, the United States have, within twenty years, increased their supplies of iron and steel from 30 per cent. to over 70 per cent. of the whole quantity imported into the Dominion, and there is reason to suppose that a great part of the difference between these two proportions has been dumped material.

The effect of dumping has thus been to reduce the consumption of certain descriptions of British-made iron and steel, both in domestic and colonial markets. To those concerned in the domestic market this reduction is a matter of much concern, because it is manifest that by so much as we import foreign material into that market do we reduce the quantity of those descriptions of home-made iron and steel that would be consumed. There is no equally palpable evidence that our exports of manufactured descriptions would be any less than they are if we had no dumped material available, but depended entirely on crude materials of home origin, although it has been presumed that the supply of such materials by foreign countries has helped us to secure or to retain foreign markets for finished materials.

INTERNATIONAL COMPETITION IN THE IRON
AND STEEL TRADES

The present and the future status of the British iron trade is largely affected and must be more or less controlled by the extent and the character of the competition to which it is exposed by other countries. This must be the case, both absolutely and relatively. Much alarm has been expressed in certain quarters on account of the rapid and considerable expansion of the means of producing iron and steel in other countries. A moment's reflection, however, will show that such expansion does not necessarily involve any detriment to British trade, because the whole increase of output might possibly be absorbed in the home markets. As a matter of fact, in the case of nearly all other countries except Germany, only a relatively small part of the increase of production in iron and steel has found its way into outside markets. In the case of the United States less than 5 per cent. of the total increased output of the last ten years has been sent abroad. In the case of Germany the proportion has been very much greater, as we shall see. In the case of France and Belgium the increase of output has been pretty evenly divided between the home market and foreign sources of demand. Austria-Hungary, Russia, Italy, and Spain have all considerably increased their output of iron, but only a fractional part of such increase has been sent beyond their own frontiers. On the whole, therefore, it comes to this, that effective foreign competition in the present is practically limited to Germany and the United States, and it is for that reason that the circumstances of these two countries require to be here specially considered.

The United States

In a paper which I read in 1902, I set out that the essential differences between British and American iron-making conditions were mainly the following :—[1]

ORES :— *British.*	*American.*
Large quantities of lean.	Small supplies of lean.
Small quantity of rich.	Large supplies of rich.
Mostly mined by shafts.	Largely mined by quarrying.
Ore-field close to coal.	Ore-field remote from coal.
Coal carried to ores.	Ore carried to coal.
Transport mainly by rail.	Transport mainly by water.
FUEL :—	
Mostly within 30 miles of furnaces.	Close to furnaces in South ; 50 to 500 miles in Middle and Eastern States.
Coke getting dearer and more scarce.	Coke still cheap in South ; getting dearer elsewhere.
Supplies still adequate, but scarcity likely in 50 years.	No sign of scarcity.
BLAST FURNACES :—	
Mostly within 20 miles of sea.	Mostly in W. Pennsylvania, 400 to 500 miles from sea.
Furnaces generally of small dimensions.	Furnaces generally of large dimensions.
Average output per year per furnace, about 25,000 tons.	Average annual output per furnace, 60,000 tons.
Usual pressure of blast, 4 to 6 lb.	Blast pressure, 10 to 20 lb.
Average ore consumption per ton of pig, about 2½ tons.	Average ore consumption per ton of pig, 1¾ tons.
Average labour cost of pig at furnaces, 3s. 6d. to 4s.	Average labour cost, 2s. to 2s. 6d.
Small volume of blast.	Large volume of blast.
Furnaces have long life.	Furnaces have short life.
Average percentage of iron in home ore, about 38 per cent.	Average percentage of iron in home ore, 50 per cent.

[1] *South Staffordshire Iron and Steel Institute Proceedings* for Dec., 1902.

The adept in such questions will be able to compute from the above comparison what are the natural conditions under which the business of ironmaking is carried on in the two countries. He will also understand that the cost at which pig iron can be produced is the basis of ultimate success or failure in all ulterior branches of manufacture.

In addition, however, to the natural conditions above set forth, there are more or less artificial conditions which have played a hardly less prominent part in building up the immense fabric of the American iron industry. Natural conditions cannot readily, if at all, be reproduced in another country. Artificial conditions may be, and hence their importance is obvious, if not paramount.

The more prominent artificial conditions that have been established in the American iron industry are the following, as nearly as possible in the order of what is believed to be their relative importance :—

1. The maintenance of a high-tariff system, whereby control of the home market is secured under normal circumstances.

[NOTE.—Of course there are years when abnormal circumstances are the rule, and when, therefore—as in 1902 and 1903—home supplies have to be supplemented to a greater or less extent by imports.]

2. The consolidation of a large number of important mines and works under one control, whereby economy of production is secured within wide limits.

3. A benevolent attitude towards such economy on the part of labour, and a general readiness to take up and make the most of new methods, processes, and plant.

4. A readiness on the part of manufacturers and employers to undertake heavy capital expenditure, with a view to securing large outputs and maximum economy of labour.

5. A minimum range of standing charges, brought about by concentration of effort and policy on the problem of keeping works running full time.

6. Economy of transport, secured by running large train-loads, and using rolling stock of exceptional capacity.

7. The widely diffused application of the premium system, whereby the maximum of efficiency is got out of a given supply of labour.

8. The large and rapid increase in home consumption, which has practically doubled within the last ten years, and by which capitalists are encouraged to provide the newest and most economical and efficient systems, regardless of cost.

While these conditions are the controlling factors of the situation, the whole problem of effective competition, as already indicated, is reduced to the question of the normal price at which the competing countries can produce a ton of pig iron. Some remarks are made elsewhere on this question, and it is only necessary to add here that while the U.S. Steel Corporation can, if capital obligations be disregarded, generally produce iron cheaper than either Great Britain or any other country, under such circumstances as those that prevailed from 1893 to 1898, it is impossible for them to do so if they are to pay the interest on their capitalisation other than the common stock. In the United States, as in other countries, the value of raw materials is persistently moving towards a higher level, and care is taken to avoid a recurrence of conditions that entailed much suffering on every interest involved.

The controlling factor in the American iron industry is the extent and value of the iron ores of the Lake Superior region. Those ores provide over four-fifths of the total iron output of the United States. The situation of their supply is unique in this respect, that they have to be brought a greater distance for blast-furnace use than any other ores used on an extensive scale in the whole iron-making world.

The iron - ore supplies of the United States were cheapened and improved by the development about twelve years ago of the Mesabi range, which, from a trackless waste in 1891, was opened up by railway in 1892, produced nearly 3,000,000 tons of ore in 1895, had raised well on to 5,000,000 tons in 1898, and in 1904 had turned out over 12,000,000 tons, making it the most productive iron-ore field in the world.

The proportions of the total iron-ore output of the United States contributed by the Lake Superior region at different dates were as follows, in thousands of tons :—

Year.		Total output U.S.		Total output Lake Superior ranges.		Percentage of total supplied by Lake Superior.
1880	.	7,120	...	1,987	...	27·91
1885	.	7,600	...	2,466	...	32·45
1890	.	16,036	...	7,071	...	44·09
1895	.	15,957	...	10,429	...	65·36
1900	.	28,887	...	20,589	...	71·49
1902	.	35,554	...	26,200	...	74·90
1904	.	27,600	...	21,823	...	79.00

The American iron industry mines the bulk of the Lake Superior ores very cheaply. In a number of cases the actual cost of mining and placing on trucks a 60 per cent. ore does not exceed a shilling a ton. In no other case that I know of is this economic result attained, although Canada has the advantage of cheap ores at the Dominion Iron Works of Cape Breton, and Spain has unusually cheap ores at Bilbao and one or two other centres—in both cases at least 10 per cent. below the

Lake Superior standard. No cheap iron ores of equal quality are mined in Great Britain.

The United States has the further advantage of cheap supplies of coal available for coking, especially in the Connellsville (Pennsylvania) and West Virginia coal-fields. The coke made in these regions has been produced and sold on a considerable scale at about four shillings per ton at the ovens, which means six shillings to seven shillings per ton at the blast furnaces; but the more normal price is six shillings to eight shillings per ton at the ovens, and for the last two years the average has exceeded even the latter figure.

The primacy of the iron trade is likely to remain with the United States, for the reasons just stated. Whether the primacy of volume of output and cheapness of production will also involve primacy in foreign trade remains to be seen. The export business of that country, since it assumed any dimensions some six years ago, has fluctuated very greatly, and for the years 1902 and 1903 it was comparatively unimportant.

A question that requires attention from those who want to make a forecast of the future is that of whether British steel - manufacturers are likely to be prepared to adopt American methods and machinery on a larger scale, and whether, if they did so, their competition would be more effective than it now is. It is possible that the Americans have been too radical, while the British have been too conservative. It has been said that the Americans would spend £1,000 in order to dispense with one man. British engineers do not hesitate to declare that they could grapple with the problems involved in laying down the newest machinery and applying the best methods if only steel-manufacturers would face the cost.

American machinery has of late years been helpful in modernising and economising our processes of manufacture in many different lines of production. The danger is that its use may create a prejudice in its favour, as against English machinery, that may be unfair and detrimental to English producers, and that American plant will thus have found on this side of the Atlantic a settled home. During the last five years we have imported into this country more than £13,500,000 sterling worth of American machinery. These figures represent a larger business than has ever before been done within the same interval in the international trade relations of any two countries in the item of machinery alone. Over this interval, also, we have drawn machinery direct from Germany to the extent of £2,438,000 sterling, and through Holland—mainly from Germany—to the extent of £1,009,000. In the first year of the series our machinery imports from Germany and Holland were valued at £477,000, while in the last of the series the value had risen to £1,039,000.

GERMANY

The iron trade of the German Empire is mainly carried on in two localities that are remote from each other, the first in general importance being Rhineland Westphalia, and the second being the district which embraces Lorraine, the Saar, and Luxembourg. Each of these two regions produces about the same annual output of pig iron. Unitedly they produced in 1902 over 6,570,000 tons of pig iron, or about 79 per cent. of the total of the Empire in that year.

The ores available for the purposes of the German iron industry are chiefly mined in Alsace-Lorraine and Luxembourg. Of the 18,000,000 tons mined in the Empire in 1902, about 80 per cent. was mined in these two districts. About 4,000,000 tons of ore were imported, so that of the total consumption, reaching about 22,000,000 tons, not more than 13 per cent. was raised in other parts of Germany than the two regions already specified.

The problem of the past, present, and future of the German iron industry is, therefore, to a large extent, bound up with the development of those two regions, and almost wholly associated with those regions plus outside supplies.

So far as coke supplies are concerned, the Westphalian (Dortmund) coal-field supplies about three-fourths of the whole. The coke here produced has much about the same range of prices as that produced in the coal-fields of South Durham and South and West Yorkshire in England, but the more general adoption of by-product ovens by German coke-manufacturers gives them a material advantage in respect of cost.

The ores of Alsace and Luxembourg are very cheaply produced. Their average value at the mines over the last ten years has been officially computed at less than 2s. 6d. per ton, the ore averaging over 30 per cent. of iron. This compares not unfavourably with the general range of the oolitic ores produced in Great Britain, having a similar iron percentage; but while the ores of Cleveland, Lincolnshire, and Northamptonshire in Great Britain rarely exceed 1s. 6d. per ton for transport to blast furnaces, those of Alsace and Luxembourg cost from 6s. to 7s. per ton for transport to Westphalia, where fully one-half of them are used. Conversely, the coke of Westphalia costs about the same figure when transported to the blast furnaces of Alsace and Luxembourg.

Still more important in some respects are the conditions that obtain in differentiating the characters and qualities of German and British pig iron. More than 70 per cent. of the total output of German iron is of the basic variety, while less than 20 per cent. of the total make of British pig is in this category. The main resulting difference is that Great Britain produces more than 3,500,000 tons of hematite iron, against less than 400,000 tons of this description produced in Germany. Speaking generally, Bessemer or hematite iron costs several shillings per ton more to produce than basic iron, and to this extent it would seem as though Germany had an obvious advantage, which is lost to our own country for the reasons already stated.

This advantage, however, is being more or less countervailed by the increasing necessity for importing foreign ores into the German ironmaking districts. Such ores can be imported into Great Britain at least as cheaply as into any part of Germany. In the former case the ore has only to be delivered direct into a British port; but in the case of German works, the ore has to be carried up the Rhine for more than a hundred miles, and then transhipped for land transport to blast furnaces, most of which are several miles inland.

Speaking generally, there does not seem to be any advantage enjoyed by Germany which may not be equalled, if not excelled, by the iron trade of Great Britain, while the quoted prices of pig iron in German markets are almost invariably higher than the quotations for British pig iron of the same quality in British markets.

Nevertheless, the German iron industry has during recent years undertaken and carried out a development alike in output and in exports, to which the history of the British iron trade can furnish no parallel. During the last ten years the make of German pig iron has more than doubled. Within the same interval, the output of German steel has increased from 3,163,000 tons to nearly 8,500,000 tons, or an increase of 174 per cent.

A very large part of this increase has been shipped to foreign countries and British colonies. The total exports in the ten years have increased nearly threefold, and the total volume of German iron and steel exports in 1903 was nearly equal to that of Great Britain.

A very large proportion of this great increase has been shipped to British home and colonial markets, which in the years 1902–3 absorbed nearly a million tons of German iron and steel per annum.

The competitive conditions under which these results have been achieved are somewhat recondite and complex. It would be too much to assert that they have entirely been due to dumping—that is, to selling at high prices at home, in order to cover sales at low prices abroad—but this has undoubtedly been a large factor in the business situation. It is hardly necessary to add that this is not competition of the ordinary and reasonable kind that can be met by a parity of conditions, having regard to the wide differences in the fiscal systems of the two countries.

OTHER COUNTRIES

While it is possible to say a good deal as to the competition of some other countries, based on their resources and prospects, no such present competition exists to a very material extent, except in the case of Belgium, whose exports of iron are, however, very small compared with those of Great Britain, Germany, and the United States. Belgium, as we have seen,[1] has only limited resources, and her competition is hardly likely to assume much greater proportions than at present. Sweden is also a relatively unimportant competitor. As yet, no other country can be said to compete at all.

[1] *Op. cit.*, p. 87.

CHAPTER XVII

PRICES AND PROFITS IN THE IRON INDUSTRY

IT is natural for the average man, unacquainted with all the technical conditions and commercial vicissitudes that affect the business, to assume that ironmaking is one of the most profitable of occupations. There is some reason for this assumption. As a general rule it may be taken for granted that where there are great fluctuations of price, and notable differences of conditions, there are great possibilities of loss on the one hand and profit on the other. There is no business of which this is more true than that of manufacturing iron and steel. How shall we proceed to estimate the average results of the business? That is a necessary, but it it is also a complex and difficult branch of inquiry. The circumstances of an individual enterprise do not afford any reliable criterion of those of the trade as a whole. You cannot apply the rule of *ex uno disce omnes*. Even in the most prosperous of times, some concerns make heavy losses, and equally under the most depressed conditions of the trade, others make considerable profits.

The capacity of an ironmaking or steel-manufacturing plant to yield profits of greater or less amount depends primarily upon its command of cheap raw material; secondly, upon its command of cheap transportation; and in the third place, upon its having effective labour at a reasonable, but not necessarily a nominally cheap cost.

In all manufacturing countries iron and steel plants may be divided into the two categories of those that have their own raw materials and those that have not. There have been periods when it was not regarded as much of an advantage to possess iron and coal mines and coking plants. In two or three periods within the last thirty years, both iron ore and coal have been purchased for less than the general cost of production, and that over a considerable time. There are increased responsibilities and risks attending the possession and working of mines and collieries, which often render them a doubtful gain. In such cases—unhappily not infrequent—as that of a serious strike, the mine-owner would often wish to throw off his burden of care, and if he is also an ironmaster he will probably, in any case, have to obtain his supplies of material elsewhere while the strike is in progress. I can remember occasions in the North of England, for example, when the ironmasters of Cleveland who owned ironstone mines had to buy their ores in Lincolnshire and elsewhere, and when the owners of collieries and coke-ovens in South Durham had to purchase supplies of both in South and West Yorkshire, owing to local differences and the stoppage of local sources of supply.

Of late years, however, it has become increasingly recognised that the pig-iron-maker is in a more desirable situation when he controls his supplies of raw materials through the prerogatives of direct ownership. Where the steel-manufacturer controls both his raw materials and his pig-iron supplies in the same way, his position is theoretically ideal. In such cases, the profits that had formerly to be paid at each step along the line on coal, coke, iron ore, limestone, etc., become merged in one profit. It no longer happens that the blast-furnace owner must pay a profit to the mine-owner, to the colliery-owner, and to the coke-manufacturer, nor must the steel-producer pay a profit to the maker of pig iron, nor the rolling-mill proprietor pay a profit to the Bessemer and open-hearth steel producer, who provides his supply of blooms and billets. Under the newest and now more general arrangements which regulate and control everyday practice, the intermediate profits are treated as a final profit on the finished product. Where this happens, the total profit is naturally as a rule greater than any of the individual profits, and the producer is thereby left in a better competitive position and can produce more cheaply in times of stress and strain.

In Great Britain ironworks and steelworks may be divided into the two categories of those that pay good profits and those that pay either small profits or none at all. On a balance of the whole, it is probable that there is about the same number of establishments in each of these categories. The best-paying works, as a rule, are those that have made a feature of specialities that are not too keenly competed for, in respect of which special knowledge is required, and for the prosecution of which exceptional plant is required. There are a number of such concerns in Sheffield and its neighbourhood. Another group of plants yield exceptionally satisfactory results because of their exceptional command of raw materials, and still another, because the capitalisation has been kept down to a low figure, and liberal depreciation provided for. The antithesis of these conditions generally leaves the concern involved in a more or less unsatisfactory situation. Such a situation is created in some cases by an unsuitable and unfavourable location, as, for example, where high railway rates are charged either to secure supplies of materials or to get manufactured products to market. From this latter point of view, Cleveland, the Glasgow district, and South Wales provide more or less the ideal situations, while South and North Staffordshire, Shropshire, and Northamptonshire, provide conditions of a more or less opposite kind. Other districts, such as West Cumberland, possess excellent shipping conditions, but stand at a serious disadvantage in respect of access to raw materials.

In all cases alike profits vary from year to year, and in practically every case profits are sometimes made, although here and there they are like the proverbial angels' visits. It is very surprising how long a business may be carried on without making any distribution of profits. In our own country cases are not unknown where no dividends have been paid for fifteen years. And yet, while this was the persistent experience of one enterprise, another, not so far away, has been dividing profits every year, made in the same branches of manufacture.

The question is sometimes raised whether a country like our own, with a free-trade system, is not placed at a disadvantage in comparison with competitive countries which enjoy the advantages of protection. The study of this problem is interesting, but space will not allow me to pursue it here. Suffice it to say that there is no uniform conclusion to be drawn by a study of comparative profits in favour of either the one system or the other. As great profits and as great losses in carrying on the iron and steel industries have been made in protectionist as in free-trade countries. In the case of Germany, for example, out of thirty-five works engaged in the iron and steel industries in 1901–2, no fewer than seventeen paid no dividends at all, while in the following year out of the same number of firms, eleven paid no dividends. In the same years, however, other concerns paid dividends up to 32 per cent. In the case of the United States the profits made in the iron trade have, generally speaking, been greater than those paid in either of the other two countries dealt with, but even here there have been long

N

periods, as in the years 1892–8, when profits have been almost a minus quantity except to the favoured few.

A recent report of the Metz Chamber of Commerce deals with the German iron and steel trades in the following terms :—

" The condition of the iron and steel industries has been as unfavourable as it was in 1902. The domestic demand did not absorb more than 50 per cent. of the production, and it would have been impossible to get rid of the other half had not the United States come up as a customer. The prices obtained on the exports netted a severe loss, as the cost of production was high, owing to dear coal. The prospects for 1904 are even more dismal, as there are signs apparent that the United States has changed its rôle of a customer to that of a competitor, and it is only a question of time when that Republic will enter the world's market as a large seller of iron and steel products."

The variations in profits, like the fluctuations in price, may be traced in the Stock Exchange quotations for iron properties. Here are some such values in the case of German establishments, mostly of the first rank :—

	1900.		1901.
Hasper Eisen and Stahlwerke	455	...	110
Hagener Gussstahlwerke	145	...	46
Gelsenkirchener Bergwerk	230	...	153
Geisweider Eisenwerk	360	...	129
Dusseldorf Eisenhütten G.	289	...	108
Dortmunder Union	141	...	44
Bismarckhütte	340	...	160
Eschweiler	276	...	72
Bochum	283	...	157

This list could be largely added to, in regard alike to coal and iron. One of the most remarkable cases is that of the Schalker Gruben-u.-Hüttenverein—a large colliery enterprise—whose shares fell in this interval from 800 to 239 marks.

It has been shown that the general organisation of industry on the trust system fails to either enable the companies syndicated to maintain their rates of profit or to conserve the value of their property. It is true that many syndicated companies have paid handsome dividends, but so also have many British firms in the same business, without the artificial aid of trusts and syndicates.

It is clear that in so far as the cost of pig iron is a safe criterion, the price of British pig iron enables the British steel manufacturer to secure larger profits than those to be earned in either Germany or the United States, assuming approximately the same realised prices for the finished products.

The difference between the cost of production and the realised selling price is usually assumed to be profit, and so in a sense it is; but it is not always divisible profit. Before dividends can be paid, interest obligations, depreciation, renewals, reserves, and other charges have to be met, and these in some cases absorb much larger percentage proportions of the gross profit than in others. Subject to this understanding, the following figures, recently published on the Continent, give what I consider a possible approximation to the costs and profits of the German iron trade in 1903 :—

GERMAN COSTS AND SELLING PRICES IN 1903—WEST-PHALIA DISTRICT. IN MARKS OR SHILLINGS PER TON

	Cost of Production.	Cartel Home Selling Prices.	Export Prices.
Thomas iron .	38·15 to 46·80 ...	57·40 to 58·10	——
Acid pig .	36·50 „ 45·50 ...	56·00	——

GERMAN COSTS AND SELLING PRICES IN 1903—WESTPHALIA
DISTRICT. IN MARKS OR SHILLINGS PER TON—*continued*

	Cost of Production.		Cartel Home Selling Prices.	Export Prices.
Basic ingots	50·48 to	59·35 ...	77·20	... 70 to 73
Siemens acid do.	60·55 „	65·55		
Basic blooms .	59·30 „	69·90 ...	82·50	... ———
„ billets .	65·90 „	77·25 ...	90·00	... 72 to 80
„ girders .	71·65 „	83·75 ...	100·00 to 105·00	... 78 „ 83
„ rails .	73·00 „	84·85 ...	105	... 78 „ 88
„ plates .	90·65 „	102·50 ...	115	... 107·50*
Acid bars .	70·10 „	76·90 ...	92·50	... 77·50*
„ plates .	103·00 „	110·90 ...	120·00	... ———

Some further idea of the differences in the dividend-
paying capabilities of different plants, with and without
their own mineral supplies, may be got from the following
estimates, which have recently been made on good authority for Westphalia :—

Description of Pig.	Cost in works with their own ore-mines and cokeries, and using hot metal. Shillings per ton.		Cost where ore and coke are bought and blooms are reheated. Shillings per ton.
Basic iron .	. . 36·00	...	40·60
Ingots .	. . 48·95	...	53·30
Blooms .	. . 56·65	...	64·30
Billets .	. . 64·15	...	74·95
Girders .	. . 70·20	...	81·35
Rails .	. . 71·65	...	82·65
Plates .	. . 91·85	...	102·65

On the subject of the future conditions of demand and
distribution it may be remarked that experience has
proved that domestic consumption cannot long be continued on a large scale on prices far above the normal

* Antwerp.

level. In every ten years in the past there have been one or two years of boom, three or four years of normal business, and four or five years of depression. While it is probably impossible to avoid the massing of demand in certain years, when the most favourable conditions prevail, and to prevent the advance of prices that follows, it is the universal testimony of makers that those boom years are as demoralising in their results as the years of low prices and small profits. If steady and normal markets be the desire of all, and if the only monopoly in iron and steel manufacture that can thrive is that based on the ability to produce cheaper and sell cheaper than any other maker, it may be that the entire industry must be subjected, sooner or later, to a very radical process of reorganisation. Moderate prices are as necessary to secure and hold export trade as they are to maintain a high standard of domestic consumption, and moderate prices depend on low cost of manufacture. The United States are paying nearly three times the wages of their most vigorous rival, and about double the wages of their next strongest competitor, while only "a rash enthusiast" would place the superiority of American labour as high as 50 per cent.

It is a matter of common knowledge and complaint that the high prices now, and for several years past, paid for raw materials, and more especially for coal and pig iron, render the course of the manufacture of finished materials, such as bars, rails, and plates, anything but smooth. But while this is true, the margin of difference in favour of the manufacturer of finished products was for a time greater than usual.

The following short table gives the average official prices of German No. 1 foundry iron on the Essen bourse compared with Glasgow warrants and United States foundry iron at Pittsburg, showing, for the later years more especially, a notable difference of price in favour of the Scotch product :—

AVERAGE PRICES OF GERMAN, SCOTCH, AND
AMERICAN FOUNDRY PIG

	German Foundry, No. 1.			Glasgow Warrants.			American Foundry, No. 1 at Philadelphia.	
	£	s.		£	s.		£	s.
1897	67	0	...	45	0	...	43	0
1898	67	0	...	47	6	...	44	6
1899	68	0	...	62	0	...	65	0
1900	96	0	...	65	0	...	78	0
1901	102	0	...	55	0	...	61	0
1902	65	0	...	54	0	...	83	0
1903	63	6	...	52	3	...	79	10
1904	60	4	...	51	5	...	63	1

So far as the United States are concerned, recently published tables of the cost, selling price, and margin of profit in steel billets during the years 1890 to 1900 show that in the first-named year the profit varied from 8s. 6d. to 18s., with a cost of production of from 96s. 6d. to 128s. 6d. The cost of production showed a steady decline till 1897-8, in which years it varied between 56s. 6d. and 66s. At this time profits were very low, and in many cases non-existent. The cost of production then increased up to 1900, when it is put down at from 80s. 6d. to 136s. For the year 1901 the cost ranged from 79s. 6d. in January to 96s. 6d. in April; the selling price from 79s. in January to 97s. 6d. in June; and the profits, which in the first four months of the year were not only *nil*, but had been converted into a loss, reached a maximum of 7s. 6d. in August.

The Industrial Commission (U.S.) reported that in 1901 the average cost of steel rails varied from 86s. in January to 104s. in April; that the selling price varied from 104s. in January to 112s. in the four months ending August 1st, and that the average margin between cost and price varied from 2s. in March and April, to 18s. in January, showing a decline of margin within a few months to the extent of 16s. per ton.

For the eleven years ending with 1900, the report of the Industrial Commission states the average cost of production, selling prices, and margin of profit for pig iron as follows :—

Year.	Average cost of production.		Selling price.				Margin of profit.			
	s.	d.	s.	d.		s.	d.	s.	d.	s.	d.
1890 .	62	0 ...	66	6 to	94	6 ...	4	6 to	32	6
1891 .	51	0 ...	60	6 „	66	0 ...	9	6 „	15	0
1892 .	53	0 ...	55	6 „	62	6 ...	2	6 „	9	6
1893 .	45	6 ...	44	9 „	55	6 ...	0	9 „	10	0
1894 .	34	6 ...	41	3 „	52	6 ...	6	9 „	18	0
1895 .	38	0 ...	40	0 „	68	6 ...	2	0 „	30	6
1896 .	48	0 ...	44	0 „	53	6 ...	4	0 „	5	6
1897 .	38	0 ...	37	9 „	43	0 ...	0	3 „	5	0
1898 .	39	0 ...	40	0 „	42	6 ...	1	0 „	3	6
1899 .	41	0 ...	44	0 „	100	0 ...	3	0 „	59	0
1900 .	61	6 ...	53	6 „	100	0 ...	8	0 „	38	6

To the prices of iron ore in the computation of costs of producing pig iron has been added 4s. per ton as representing approximately the freight rate from the lake ports to Pittsburg. During these eleven years prices of raw materials fluctuated enormously. Lake Angeline ore, which is typical, averaged 24s. per ton in 1890, and only 10s. 9d. per ton in 1897.

In 1901, the cost of producing the above iron averaged 43s. 3d., and the margin of profit varied from 9s. 3d. to 23s. 9d. per ton, the profit on pig and rails rising to 32s.

The range and conditions of profit in the iron trade have in the past been liable to be greatly affected by the introduction of new processes and methods of manufacture, whereby the costs of production have virtually been revolutionised. At one time in the United States a roller in a rail mill, rolling iron or steel rails, received about

15 cents per ton, turning out from seventy-five to one hundred tons per turn. More recently, in some of the modern steel rail mills, less than 1 cent per ton is paid for doing the same work, and yet by the end of the year the roller in the rail mill to-day can make as much money as he did when he received the above higher prices under the old method of working, and that, too, with less physical labour. At one time 45 cents per ton were paid for heating iron for making iron rails. To-day very little more than half a cent per ton is paid for doing the same work. Some twenty-five years ago a man having charge of a rod mill received $2·12 per ton of rods made, out of which he paid no help whatever. At that time 12 to 15 tons were considered a good day's work. To-day it has become almost common practice to make 200 tons of wire rods in a single turn ; and upon the basis on which rod-rollers are paid to-day, they would not receive much more than 12 cents per ton. A quarter of a century ago 80 cents per ton were paid for heating billets to make wire rods ; to-day 5 cents per ton are commonly paid, and the daily wage is higher than it was when 80 cents per ton were paid. It has been computed that if the rollers now employed at the Homestead Works of the Carnegie Steel Company were paid the same wages per ton that they were paid twenty to twenty-five years ago, they would be receiving from $200 to $250 per turn on a single day's work. On the same basis, if rod-rollers to-day were to receive the same per ton that they received at that time for a turn's work of 200 tons they would receive $424 per day, or single turn.

It will, of course, be understood that the statements here made as to the greater efficiency of iron-trade labour during recent years apply, *mutatis mutandis*, to the labour of British works and Continental countries.

CHAPTER XVIII

THE RANGE AND REGULATION OF PRICES

THE thought that is uppermost in the mind of every ironmaster and steel manufacturer, not now and then, but persistently and necessarily, is that of the future of prices. What price is he likely to get next month or next year for his staple product, whatever it may happen to be? On this depend more or less the fixing and terms of his contracts, his wage arrangements and conditions, and many other considerations that may promote success on the one hand, or failure on the other. But the iron trade is to a large extent a gamble in at least this respect—that no man can tell what a day may bring forth.

The history of prices in the iron trade has yet to be written. No Tooke has hitherto appeared to undertake such a herculean labour. And yet such a record would clearly be of great advantage to both buyers and sellers, as well as an important chapter in the commercial history of the world.

Variations of price are common to all countries, but probably they reach their meridian in the United States, where yearly differences of as much as 150 per cent. are not unknown alike for iron ore, coke, pig iron, and steel products. A comparison of the years 1895 and 1902 would show numerous variations to this extent.

The highest and lowest average prices for certain standard products at home have been within recent years as follows :—

		1895.	1900.
		£ s. d.	£ s. d.
Scotch bars	. . . .	5 0 0 ...	8 10 0
		1886.	1900.
South Staffordshire "list" iron	.	7 5 0 ...	11 10 0
Merchant bars (Liverpool)	.	4 15 0 ...	10 10 0
		1896.	1891.
Tin-plates (per box)	. . .	0 9 6 ...	0 17 6

Some fluctuations within a single twelvemonth have been very remarkable. In 1891, for example, the price of tin-plates varied from 12s. 6d. to 17s. 6d. per box. In 1899 the price of merchant bars at Liverpool varied from £6 10s. to £9 10s.

There is a not uncommon impression that the trade of the past has been steadied by the existence of large stocks of iron in warrant stores, which have for many years been a feature of the business carried on in Scotland, Cleveland, and West Cumberland. The following figures throw discredit on this assumpton :—

SCOTCH IRON WARRANTS AND STOCKS

Year.		Highest.	Lowest.	Stock in Warrant Yards.
		s. d.	s. d.	Tons.
1903	. .	57 6 ...	48 9 ...	9,290
1902	. .	58 4 ...	48 10 ...	24,035
1901	. .	58 6 ...	48 9 ...	58,324
1900	. .	77 10½ ...	59 8 ...	71,286
1899	. .	75 7 ...	49 7 ...	245,258
1898	. .	50 5 ...	45 2½ ...	316,507
1897	. .	48 11 ...	43 2 ...	337,480
1896	. .	49 3 ...	44 9½ ...	363,072
1895	. .	49 1 ...	41 0½ ...	346,003
1894	. .	40 2½ ...	41 3 ...	287,886
1893	. .	51 0 ...	43 2½ ...	381,790
1892	. .	47 0 ...	40 0 ...	443,646
1891	. .	59 0 ...	42 1½ ...	579,677
1890	. .	66 3 ...	43 4 ...	613,445
1889	. .	64 10½ ...	40 10 ...	1,035,840
1888	. .	43 6 ...	37 1 ...	1,244,433

It will be noted here that some of the greatest fluctuations and highest prices coincided with the heaviest stocks, as in 1891, 1890, and 1889. On the other hand, the low and almost nominal stocks of 1900 also fell contemporaneously with exceptionally high and greatly fluctuating prices.

In most countries the recent movement of prices has, on the whole, been in an upward direction. The period during which there was a fairly steady movement to a lower level may be regarded as having ended about 1896, when the last considerable trade revival set in. In the interval between that period and the present date, prices have in many cases fallen to nearly their former level; but this does not apply to raw materials, nor does it generally apply to pig iron, which are the ultimate controlling factors in the iron trade. The prices of finished products have consequently been disproportionately low over a wide range of operations, and profits have been small, although in a number of cases economies in production have caused the disparity to be more or less compensated.

I have found that in some quarters there is a disposition to regard Great Britain as specially subject to serious variations of price. Perhaps the conditions under which our iron markets are carried on tend to frequent and often considerable fluctuations; but I am not aware that the range or incidence of these changes are more serious than those that occur in other countries. With a view to bringing this matter to a test, I have prepared the two tables that follow—the first showing the official average prices of coal, iron ore, iron, and steel in Germany since 1860; and the second showing a comparison of German prices in the low-price year 1894 and in the high-price year 1900 :—

AVERAGE OFFICIAL PRICES OF GERMAN PRODUCTS IN MARKS AND DECIMALS THEREOF, PER TON

Year.	Coal.	Iron Ore.	Pig Iron.	Finished Iron.	Finished Steel.
1860	5·35	5·52	125·35	—	—
1870	6·19	6·28	76·24	—	—
1875	7·95	5·66	74·21	156·49	242·75
1880	5·23	4·76	59·87	151·36	207·54
1885	5·23	3·70	43·65	124·84	147·44
1890	7·66	4·19	57·44	153·04	166·83
1895	6·85	3·32	43·36	115·97	117·45
1900	8·84	4·09	64·68	180·15	165·45
1902	8·85	3·66	53·42	136·11	128·99
1904	8·50	3·40	43·04	132·01	125·20

AVERAGE ANNUAL PRICES OF IRON AND STEEL AT GERMAN (WESTPHALIAN) WORKS, DISTINGUISHING HIGHEST PRICES FROM LOWEST PRICES, IN THE YEARS 1894 AND 1900 [1]

Description.	1894.	1900.	Increase in year 1900. Range.	Percentage.
PIG IRON:—	s.	s.	s.	
No. 1 foundry	58·33	93·00	34·67	59·43
No. 3 foundry	52·00	95·00	43·00	82·69
English foundry	52·12	90·84	38·72	74·48
Luxembourg foundry	38·22	85·00	46·78	122·23
Bessemer pig	52·00	91·00	39·00	75·00
Forge pig	45·58	85·00	39·42	86·48
Basic pig	45·17	90·20	45·03	99·69
Spiegel	49·61	72·10	22·49	45·33
OTHER IRON AND STEEL:—				
Bar iron	96·25	185·00	88·75	92·20
Boiler plates	148·88	210·20	61·32	41·18
Tank plates	122·22	200·42	78·20	63·98
Sheets	115·72	252·50	136·78	118·19

So far as American products are concerned, the official records show that the average price of Bessemer pig iron at Pittsburg has advanced from about ten dollars to nearly

[1] The year 1900 is selected because it was a period of high prices for most iron and steel products.

thirty dollars per ton, and other grades have more or less followed suit. The range of fluctuation in pig iron has, on the whole, been greater than that which has occurred in reference to finished products, although here also there have been considerable variations even within a couple of years, as the following short table of average prices at works will show :—

	1897.		1899.		Increase in 1899.
	cents.		cents.		cents.
Bar iron	1·11	...	1·80	...	·69
Soft steel bars . .	1·13	...	1·90	...	·77
Angles	1·19	...	2·00	...	·81
Smooth machinery steel .	1·53	...	2·50	...	·97
Open-hearth spring steel .	1·66	...	2·85	...	1·19

It is likely to be of interest if I supplement this short table by an approximate record of the comparative prices of leading products at different dates. This is attempted in the next two tables :—

AVERAGE PRICES OF LEADING DESCRIPTIONS OF IRON IN GREAT BRITAIN

	1880.			1890.			1900.		
	£	s.	d.	£	s.	d.	£	s.	d.
Scotch warrants . .	2	4	4	...	2	3	4	...	2	19	8
Scotch bars . .	6	10	0	...	7	0	0	...	8	10	0
Merchant bars, Liverpool	5	15	0	...	6	0	0	...	9	10	0
S. Staffordshire List iron	7	15	0	...	9	5	0	...	10	15	0

AVERAGE PRICE PER TON OF PIG IRON PRODUCED BY MINERAL FUEL IN THE UNITED STATES IN 1880, 1890, AND 1900, IN DOLLARS AND CENTS

	1880.		1890.		1900.
Pennsylvania .	25·85	...	17·28	...	14·97
Ohio .	26·04	...	16·36	...	15·73
Illinois .	28·06	...	15.20	...	10·23
New Jersey .	24·27	...	17·21	...	16·81
Alabama .	22·69	...	11·65	...	10·96
W. Virginia .	22·48	...	17·39	...	16·57
Tennessee .	17.25	...	12·38	...	12·10

An examination of these figures will show that the average recorded value at the furnaces had greatly fallen in every one of the States enumerated over this period, in some cases by more than one-half. The drop in the cases of Illinois and Alabama is more especially remarkable, and not less so because the former State has neither ores nor fuel close at hand, while the latter has both to a large extent within a ring fence. The greatest fall took place between the years 1880 and 1890. Between 1890 and 1900, however, there were much lower values than those recorded for the latter years.

No fall in prices that has occurred within recent years has been more notable than that which occurred in the United States in 1903–4. Comparing the prices of March, 1904, with the same month of 1903, there was a drop which varied from 15 to 50 per cent. all round. The greatest fluctuations took place in steel billets (42 per cent.), old car-wheels (47·9 per cent.), gray forge iron (37·5 per cent.), foundry pig iron (42·4 per cent.), and Lake Superior charcoal iron (54·2 per cent.). In some of these cases the difference of price was as much as 46s. per ton. This remarkable movement has coincided with the utmost efforts of the Steel Corporation to maintain the general level.

During the life of the Steel Corporation the fluctuations of price in iron and steel products have been as great as they ever were at any previous time. Within thirteen months of the years 1902–3 the price of No. 1 foundry iron at Philadelphia varied by as much as 37s. 6d. per ton; the price of gray forge iron by 34s. 4d.; the price of Bessemer iron by 38s.; and the price of steel billets by 37s. 6d. per ton. These are fluctuations that have rarely been equalled in amount within a similarly short period, whether in the United States or in any other country.

We have now seen that the fluctuations of price in all leading iron-producing countries are considerable, that no one country appears to suffer more than another, that the efforts of manufacturers by organisation on a large scale, as in the cases of the U.S. Steel Corporation and of the German Steel Combine, have not been successful in avoiding them, or even in greatly modifying the conditions under which they occur ; and we may here further add that price fluctuations are perhaps more often than not unanticipated and unlooked for, that they generally come suddenly and without much warning, that they are often due to " bear " or " bull " operations, as distinguished from legitimate demand, and that their duration is as much a matter incapable of measurement as the time of their happening.

> If merchant could one day foresee,
> He would no longer merchant be.

The competency of combinations of manufacturers to regulate prices has, however, been proved, under some conditions, to be exceptional and important. Take, as a case in point, the uniformity secured for steel rail prices during the life of the Steel Rail Manufacturers' Association in 1880-1, and the steadiness with which rail prices have been maintained in the United States in the period 1902-5. There are other cases of a similar character. In nearly all such cases the essentials required are a sufficient number of assents, and protection from outside competition. In the first of the cases above named, the combination was an international one, and each country's manufacture was limited as to output. In the second case, the success of the movement was due to the limited number of assents required and the controlling influence of the Steel Corporation. Several rail manufacturers' combinations have been maintained in Great Britain for a

short time, and so with other organisations designed to
regulate the prices and production of products in the
making of which there were only a few firms concerned.

The experience of the United States in 1903, despite
the existence of the Steel Corporation, which was expected
to steady prices, has been very remarkable from this point
of view.   Within twelve months, three notable things
happened—(1) the general rate of output of pig iron and
steel was reduced by nearly one-half; (2) the prices of
both raw materials and manufactured products fell by
nearly one-half; and (3) the shares of the leading iron and
steel manufacturing companies suffered a fall which ranged
from 20 per cent. to 60 per cent.   Great Britain has in
recent years had no such severe experience.   The conditions of Germany in 1901 were probably, on the whole,
worse than those of the United States in 1903.

One of the greatest wants of the iron trade, both at home
and abroad, is an influence, method, or arrangement whereby prices may be steadied, and violent fluctuations of production, prices, and foreign business obviated.   Much has
been attempted in this direction, but so far with but little
success.   We have seen that in the United States it was
hoped, and by many apparently believed, that the nearest
possible approach to a perfect cure had been provided by
the establishment of the Steel Corporation, controlling,
as it did, over one-half of the output of that country in
raw materials and in finished products.   But these hopes
and beliefs have so far been disappointed.   The most
violent fluctuations of all kinds have happened under the
Steel Corporation *régime*.   The output of iron ore had
declined by more than one-third.   The output of pig iron
for a short time had declined by nearly one-half.   The
prices of iron ore and coke fell by 30 per cent.   Prices of
finished materials were reduced all round, and competitive
conditions were forced upon the trade which had hardly

been paralleled for severity and persistency in the worst days of the many previous periods of cut-throat competition. Not only so, but the very life of the Steel Corporation has been threatened. The value of its shares and stocks has fallen enormously. It has lately been threatened with default in respect to all its obligations. No one now appears to attach much importance to its future influence as a means of steadying the trade.

So far as the future is concerned, there is a probability that the influence of the Steel Corporation will be more and more strongly exerted in the United States to maintain prices, as it has hitherto been. If they succeed, it will probably be fortunate for British trade. At the level of price maintained for the last two or three years, most British works can undersell the American product, both in home and colonial markets. I do not, of course, assume that this will follow if dumping on a large scale is resorted to.

CHAPTER XIX

TRUSTS, CARTELS, AND SYNDICATES

THE greatest home of the cartel and the syndicate is Germany. Most commodities produced there on a large scale have their own special syndicate. That is, perhaps, more true of the coal and iron trades than of any other, but at any rate, so far as these trades are concerned there is a syndicate for every article that is large enough to be organised. There are coal, lignite, coke, and briquette syndicates ; pig iron, foundry products, finished iron, and steel syndicates; trusts also for steel forgings, steel castings, wire, old iron, pipes and tubes, rails, plates, sheets, girders, and other products. And not only so, but district syndicates exist in a number of cases, so that there is more than one organisation for the same product. Coal, for example, is under the control of four syndicates—in Rhineland-Westphalia, in Upper and in Lower Silesia, and in Zwickau-Oelsnitz. The pig-iron trade is regulated by separate trusts in Rhineland-Westphalia, in Lorraine-Luxembourg, in Siegerland, and in Upper Silesia. Plates and sheets are controlled by separate syndicates, besides four other syndicates for rolling-mill products generally. Wire, again, is under regulation by three different syndicates, briquettes by three, blooms and billets by two, and so on. A recently published list gave particulars of forty-six different syndicates in the German coal and iron trades alone.

194

The three greatest trusts or combinations in the iron trade of to-day are:—

1. The United States Steel Corporation, which controls about 270 different iron and steel manufacturing plants, employs about 160,000 workmen, and has a capital of £300,000,000 sterling.

2. The German Steel Syndicate, which embraces all but 10 per cent. of the great steel-manufacturing plants of Germany, employs nearly 50,000 workmen, and controls the production of seven million tons of steel annually.

3. The International Rail Syndicate, which has its head-quarters in London, and is carried on to prevent the cutting of prices as between manufacturers of rails in the United Kingdom, Germany, and the United States. The members of this syndicate control an output of some four million tons of rails annually, of which the average annual export is about a million tons.

In addition to these, there are numerous smaller syndicates or organisations for the regulation of prices and production, in most ironmaking countries, including Great Britain. Indeed, there are few products of the steel industry that are not more or less regulated from these two points of view.

In all such cases, the primary purpose has been to establish such an understanding or agreement as to prices that competition in its most serious forms can be practically controlled.

In the United States, the syndicate which was the rule a few years ago has given place to the consolidation, so called, which means a union, under the same proprietary, of a greater or less number of different establishments. The greatest of these is the Steel Corporation, founded in the spring of 1901, with a capital £230,000,000 sterling, which has since then been increased to about £280,000,000, and which, in the last two years, produced nearly one-half of all the pig iron, and more than one-half of all the steel turned out in the United States. The ostensible objects of consolidation are the control of production and prices, and economy of production resulting from the cutting down of many expenses which are more or less duplicated in individual concerns.

In Germany various syndicates have in the past combined among each other in order to grant export bonuses. Thus the Semi-finished Steel Union arranged for an export bonus per ton as much as 33⅓ per cent. of the amount of ingots used from the works of the Union. Of this the Coal Syndicate bore 5s. The Pig Iron Syndicate allowed its customers an export premium of 10s. per ton ; the Merchant Iron Union at the same time created an export league for merchant iron, which fixed the prices for export upon a scale varying considerably from that for home consumption. While the Coke Syndicate asked 15s. per ton at home, it simultaneously effected heavy sales abroad at 11s. per ton. The Rail Syndicate is said to have sold rails to foreigners 30s. cheaper than to German customers. We have already spoken of the flagrant case of the Union of German Wire Manufacturers.[1] So it has been with practically all other branches of the German iron industry. Prices are kept up at home and reduced abroad. This policy not unreasonably formed the subject of a complaint addressed to the Government by the shipping yards on the Lower Rhine, declaring that they could no longer compete with Holland, which received the German material at much lower prices.

Again, the Coal Syndicate calculated for a recent year that it distributed 30,000,000 tons of coal, and granted premiums amounting to £850,000 on its normal prices for export. The courts at Gottesburg had evidence brought before them that the Coke Syndicate had sold to Austria

[1] *Op. cit.*, p. 161.

blast-furnace coke at 8*s.* 1*d.* per ton, while charging 17*s.* at home.

So far as Continental trusts are concerned, those of Germany have probably not done us so much harm as is generally supposed. Attempts have been made for some time past to establish an organisation described as an Oberreichungstelle, which is designed to reimburse German ironmasters and steel-manufacturers for the losses incurred in selling under cost price in foreign markets, but that policy has not been very successful. The German manufacturers are divided into two distinct, and more or less antagonistic, categories—the first, those who both make pig iron and manufacture steel blooms and billets for sale ; and the second, those who do not make pig iron, but buy their blooms and billets, and work them up into more finished products. The former group have for the last two years been selling blooms and billets in this country at lower prices than they have sold to the second group. This system has rendered it extremely difficult for the second group to sell in the German home market, and has made it almost impossible for them to cultivate foreign markets, because they could only do so at a loss, which their possible profits would not enable them to recoup.

In Germany the trust movement has perhaps extended as far as in the United States, and the combinations there, speaking generally, exert as great power over prices, over wages, and in other directions, as they do in America. The plan of organisation, however, is materially different. In most cases the German combinations are made simply by contracts between independent establishments regarding output, prices, etc., instead of the form being that of a single large corporation. In practically all of the important cases, however, the central control, owing to the favourable attitude of the German Government and law courts and public opinion, is such as to give full power of direction.

In Austria the situation is nearly the same, so far as the extent and power of the combinations are concerned. On the other hand, there is more disapproval of the combinations on the part of the public, and decisions of the courts made within the last few years, which render the contracts among the different parties to the combination non-enforceable, seem to have weakened the strength of the combinations within themselves.

In England the movement towards combination has not gone so far as in either Austria or Germany. There have been, at different times, many local combinations to keep up prices, and in some cases these rings have proved very successful. With the last few years, however, a very active movement towards the concentration of industry into large single corporations, after the form which has been common in the United States, may be observed. In Great Britain public opinion does not appear to be entirely favourable to the formation of great corporations formed by the buying up of many different establishments in the same line of business, corporations that through combination have succeeded in acquiring in many particulars a large degree of monopolistic control.

In France one finds the movement towards combination much less pronounced than in any of the countries just mentioned. France is less developed industrially than the other three countries, especially England and Germany; but even there the movement is making progress.

The oldest French organisation is the Comptoir Metallurgique de Longwy, which was formed in 1876 primarily to counteract the prejudice which long existed against the Minette pig, produced in Eastern France. Then the association consisted only of four works, with seven blast furnaces making forge iron, and four blast furnaces running in foundry iron, the sales for the first year being 72,000 tons. Since then the Comptoir de Longwy has become the most powerful factor in the French iron trade. Georges Villain, in a work recently issued, entitled *Le Fer, La Houille et la Metallurgie à la Fin du XIX. Siècle*, quotes some figures to show the preponderating influence upon the iron market of the Comptoir. During the first six months of 1899 there were produced outside of the department of the Meurthe-et-Moselle, of which Longwy is the commercial centre, 502,000 tons of pig iron, practically all of which was consumed in the steelworks and foundries owning the blast furnaces. There were produced during the first half of 1899, 329,000 tons of pig-iron in the Meurthe-et-Moselle by furnaces which are not controlled by the Syndicate because the iron is converted in the plants making the pig. The output of the blast furnaces, whose marketing is handled by the Comptoir, amounted to 456,000 tons. At times a considerable part of this must be exported, but this is done individually by the members, the Syndicate handling only the domestic market. Prices are regulated by a sliding scale fluctuating with the price of coke, which the furnacemen must purchase in the open market. Thus a base price is established—say, at 51·50 francs per metric ton, with coke at a cost at the furnace of 21 francs. When the price of coke rises 1 franc per ton, the price of pig iron is increased by 1·25 francs, and reductions are made in the same manner, to correspond with a decline.

The recent formation of the German Steel Syndicate has aroused Belgian producers to the necessity of doing something to help themselves in view of the constitution of such a powerful neighbour. Naturally, the success of the scheme has been watched with considerable interest, and it scarcely needed the indirect intervention of the leading Belgian banking institution—the *Société Generale* —to impress upon the Belgian ironmasters the urgency of the action. In a recent annual report the bank refers to the competition of the iron- and steel-works of adjoining countries, and suggests the desirability of a common understanding being arrived at by the home works. This advice has borne fruit, inasmuch as the reported establishment of the German Steel Syndicate was at once followed by the issue by the Ougree-Marihaye Company of invitations to the Belgian works to send representatives to attend a conference to discuss the situation of affairs. The meeting has taken place, and a favourable opinion in general was expressed in regard to the formation of a steel syndicate for Belgium.

There has been a recent tendency to form syndicates in the Russian iron trade. In the south of Russia the first negotiations were entered into towards the end of 1900, but definite action on the part of the works was only arrived at in February and May, 1902. It was then accepted in principle that the system, adopted in France, of an association for the sale of one or more particular products was best suited to Russia, and it was agreed that it was impossible to think of organising a general syndicate, embracing all kinds of manufactured iron. Accordingly, in the second half of the year 1902, a company for the sale of the iron produce of the south of Russia was started. The head office was at first located at Karkov, and subsequently, in June, 1903, transferred to St. Petersburg. It undertook the control of the trade in sheets, of which the prices during the crisis had become unduly depressed. In March, 1903, it took over the sale of girders, and in September that of axles and tyres, so that it embraced, at least for some time, these three sorts of produce. The Russian Tube Syndicate is of still earlier date. It was formed after the model of the associations of this character in Germany. It includes as members all the works producing tubes. A syndicate of the Russian nail-makers has recently been constituted.

In this case, also, the French type of association was selected. It is called the "Goozde" (the nail), and it includes twenty-eight factories out of a total of thirty-two, as well as four firms manufacturing rolled wire—exclusively for the nail trade. Other syndicates have been projected. The ironworks of the Ural districts have also made an attempt to combine, but without success. Quite recently, in the south, the formation of a pig-iron syndicate has been proposed.

Two sources of economy in the steel industries were put forward on behalf of the United States Steel Corporation—the one a saving in the cross freights, which the American Iron and Steel Company, through Mr. Gates, their president, estimated at 500,000 dollars a year, and the other due to the avoidance of changes of the rolls in rolling mills, thus abating delays which would be attended by great waste of time and energy, under the competitive system. Mr. Guthrie, the president of the American Steel Hoop Company, estimated the economy due to this latter source alone at 4s. to 6s. per ton.

The main purpose of the promoters of the Steel Corporation was to secure a more or less effective control over the conditions of production, and consequently over the movements of prices, in the United States. For this reason they had to absorb all the established companies and firms of any real importance, and paid prices for most of the plants acquired that were far in excess of their original and actual values. They did not succeed in their endeavours. Of the total recent production of iron ore in the Lake Superior region—the only American ores of any material account—under 50 per cent. was contributed by the Steel Corporation. Towards the total American production of pig iron in the same year, they contributed 45 per cent., while of the total output of all finished rolled products they provided 50 to 60 per cent.

But in certain limited departments and branches of manufacture they made a considerably better showing. They supplied 74 per cent. of the total output of Bessemer steel; 65·4 per cent. of the total output of steel rails; 58 per cent. of the total output of structural shapes; 71·6 per cent. of the total output of wire rods; 64·9 per cent. of the total production of wire nails; and 59·4 per cent. of the total output of plates and sheets. While these are in all cases vast contributions, it hardly needs to be pointed out that they are very far from giving to the Steel Corporation an effective control over any one branch of production. The fact is that the Corporation, with all its vast resources, has not held its own since its establishment. The independent manufacturers have made notably greater progress than it has done; so that the percentage proportion of the total national output now contributed by the Colossus is even less than it was. It is found that under the shelter of the influence exercised on the market by the Corporation, independent manufacturers have hitherto done very well. Their capitalisation per unit of product is not usually so large, so that at the same level of price they can make, and have made, materially larger profits.

There are two ways in which the trust system of the United States, as typified by the Steel Corporation, may prejudicially affect the trade of other countries. It may, in order to fight its home rivals and competitors, reduce prices to a point at which they find it difficult to live, and in so doing it would bring prices so much below those at which we in this country could hope to manufacture with a profit, that the American invasion would then have come in real earnest. Or it may keep up prices in the United States, which it is likely to attempt to do, and probably can succeed in doing, whether the American demand is good or bad; but failing a large home demand, it may deluge Europe with iron and steel at prices with which European countries could not hope to compete, and which would, of course, be much under the more or less regulated and artificially high prices charged to home consumers. On the other hand, it is quite possible that the Corporation may hold the power to keep up both home and foreign prices, in so far as they cultivate foreign trade at all, and that both for the sake of maintaining the high profits needed to meet their obligations, and for the sake of conciliating home con- sumers, who could not be expected to regard with equa- nimity the prospect of having to keep alive organisations of this kind by paying much higher prices for their products than those paid by foreigners. On the whole, it is clearly the interest of the Steel Corporation to keep up prices at home if they can, and it is almost equally clearly their interest not to incur public resentment and risk probable adverse legislation by cultivating foreign markets at the expense of home consumers.

The influence likely to be exercised by the Steel Corporation on the future British iron and steel trades is liable to be profoundly affected by these considera- tions.

The Corporation, as we have seen, has already failed very strikingly to realise the more prominent of the claims which were put forward on its establishment. Its financial career has recently been far from successful. It was feared that the common stock might have to be wiped out entirely. The preference shareholders may have to forego dividends for a long period. This at least is the indication afforded by the recent Stock Exchange prices of the preference stock, which could be bought at one time for about one-half of its nominal value, while the common fell to less than 10. In these circumstances the Corporation has to consider two things—what can

it do? and what should it do?   It can, of course, dump
unlimited quantities of iron and steel on outside markets
at dumping prices, but that would not be likely to help
it to pay dividends, nor would it be good policy, in view
of the attitude taken by many American consumers in
relation to tariff issues.

When in 1901 the Steel Corporation took virtual control
of the market for iron and steel products, prices were
about 70 per cent. above those of the low level of
1897.   The Trust could have raised prices, but, adopting
the theory that too rapid an advance would sooner or
later check consumption, it took orders from all and sundry
for future delivery at substantially the prices which it found
existing.   Accordingly, the mills of the Corporation were
sold months ahead, and by and by the period of delivery
became so indefinite that people who wanted quick delivery
were compelled to resort to the independent producers,
who did not happen to be sold ahead, but who exacted
a much higher price than that adhered to by the Trust.
With the slackening of the unusual demand buyers
ceased to compete for the privilege of obtaining quick
delivery of their orders, and the high prices paid for that
privilege quickly receded.   When the Steel Trust found
that it was able to take care of all the orders that were
coming into the market, the independent makers, in order
to keep their mills going, were compelled to cut under the
prices of 1901 and 1902 which were still maintained by
the Trust.   Of course, consumers resorted to the cheapest
market, which was that being made by the independent
manufacturers, while the Trust was vindicating the con-
sistency of its policy in refusing to accommodate itself to
the downward course of prices, as it had refused to follow
them to the extreme limit of their upward course.   Hence
it has been argued that the combination was not powerful
enough to keep prices at what is considered a normal level,

and to that extent the value of a considerable amount of its capitalisation had disappeared.

METHODS OF ORGANISATION IN THE IRON TRADE

There are many different methods of so organising industry as to limit competition at home and widen markets abroad, coincidently with controlling production and prices. A few of these that have been adopted and are more or less operative in the iron trade may be referred to :—

1. The system of pooling all contracts, whether on national or international lines (as in the case of the Rail Association, which flourished in Europe about twenty years ago).

2. An agreement under which each manufacturer contracts to produce only a certain volume during the year, as in the case of the German Coke Syndicate.

3. An agreement under which each manufacturer undertakes to pay an assessment on each unit exported, so that by relieving the home market of its surplus, domestic needs can be remuneratively filled.

4. Definite agreements to fix the price of the product or divide the markets, which are very common, but rarely last long.

5. The assignment of interests in different Corporations or firms concerned, to a certain number of trustees, giving power of attorney to vote the stock as they may see fit.

6. The establishment of separate Corporations, as in the case of the Standard Oil Company, under which the holders of trust certificates are given shares *pro rata* in each.

7. A voting Trust, usually applying only to one Corporation.

8. A form of organisation owning the separate plants outright, leaving the legal aspect of the new single Cor-

poration similar to that of the separate Corporations which compose it.

The subject of the organisation of industry as affecting production and prices is one that must in the future exercise a notable influence on the course of the British iron and steel trades, and it may even prove to be a dominant influence. For that reason all movement in this direction should be carefully watched. We have seen that the movement is already general and far-reaching. It has extended to practically all the more important iron-producing countries, and it has probably come to stay. The movement has elements of unquestionable strength, in so far as it secures to a large extent the maintenance of the interests of manufacturers. But it is also subject to the disintegrating and weakening influence of the op-position of consumers, who naturally resent attempts to compel them to pay artificially high prices, and will probably always be ranged on the side of the independent operator.

CHAPTER XX

THE INFLUENCE OF CUSTOMS TARIFFS ON THE IRON TRADE

THE commercial history of the iron trade is more or less an epitome of the records of tariff legislation. In no industry has such legislation played a more prominent part, during the last half-century at any rate. And this statement, which is more or less applicable to all countries, is hardly less so to Great Britain than to any other. In the earlier history of the British iron trade, tariffs were levied on a considerable scale, and as the British iron trade was then the most important, it would not be difficult to argue that it was the example of Great Britain, previous to the adoption of free trade, that led the way to the adoption of customs tariffs by other nations. It is certain that the United States, whose tariffs have been held up to anathema by all free traders for more than half a century, borrowed their system from the Mother Country, and if they did not better the instruction it was not because the Mother Country failed to provide sufficient precedents.

The most remarkable feature of British tariff history is probably the great advance that was made by the iron and other industries, not during the high-tariff period, but after all tariff duties had been removed. Free traders have been accustomed to argue that this was the result of throwing open British markets to all the world. It is possible that free trade has had something to do with the successful development of other industries, but it is difficult to see how it could have greatly influenced our commerce in iron and steel. No other country was at that period in a position to supply iron to our own on any scale of importance, because the iron industry had not in any other country assumed sufficient magnitude. Russia, Sweden, and one or two other countries, had for more than a hundred years supplied British markets with small quantities of iron and steel, but they were of too insignificant proportions to affect the general course of events, which made for a large and rapid development of the British iron trade, as such, and at the end of 1850, only a few years after free trade had become the accepted economic system of the country, left the British iron trade producing about one-half of the total iron output of the world. There is no reason to suppose that this result would not equally have happened if our previous economic system had been continued. No other country had then become sufficiently developed to either compete with or to challenge us.

If we go back to the year 1832, we find that our total exports of iron and steel then amounted to 147,636 tons, the value of which was returned at £1,190,748 tons, so that neither home nor foreign tariff duties hindered us from carrying on a considerable export business. This total was mainly made up of pig iron, bar iron, hoops, nails, rods, and castings. In the same year our imports of foreign iron exceeded 21,000 tons, mainly in the form of bars, of which considerably more than one-half was received from Sweden, mainly as a raw material of the crucible-steel industry.

Very heavy customs duties were levied on imported iron of all kinds in 1800. Bar iron had to pay a duty of £3 15s. 5d., which was raised twenty years later to £6 10s. per ton. The common impression at the time was that such duties shut out foreign iron, despite the fact that our imports of such iron were larger than our exports of British iron for nearly half a century.

The duties at that time levied on British iron imports were considerable. Pig iron paid 10*s.* per ton, bar iron 30*s.* per ton, old iron 12*s.* per ton, rods, etc., 5*s.* per hundredweight, and hoops 22*s.* 9*d.* per hundredweight. The total net revenue derived from our iron imports in the year 1800 was £21,957.

Much has been said and written of late as to the influence of tariffs and bounties on the iron and steel trades. It is largely assumed that the British steel industry is greatly handicapped by the tariff policy of foreign countries, and fears are excited as to the effect likely to be exercised by that policy on our commercial future.

The subject is a large one, and it cannot adequately be discussed in the short space available here. The case of the United States is perhaps the most instructive, as it certainly is the most prominent, as bearing on this question. The McKinley tariff of 1890, which levied a duty on imports of tin-plates nearly equal in amount to the market value of the product at the place of production, is the most notable example on record of what a hostile tariff can do to injure an established trade. Earlier tariff duties produced similar effects on other American imports.

Tariff policy, as affecting British trade, has a three-fold aspect. There is the out-and-out protectionist system, such as that practised by the United States and France; the modified tariff policy adopted by Belgium and Switzerland; and the virtual or avowed free-trade policy followed by Great Britain, Holland, and Scandinavian countries. In those countries where tariff duties are levied avowedly for the protection of home industry, care is usually taken that home producers secure practically all the home trade that is worth having, but even then they cannot

P

entirely dispense with the outside contributions which it is the business of the tariff to exclude. The Germans, for example, have until within the last year or two imported considerable quantities of British pig iron, despite the tariff, and the Americans are still importing from 60,000 to 70,000 tons of tin-plates annually, and certain other products on which high tariff duties are levied.

I have endeavoured to show elsewhere that the levy of customs duties, even when they are on a tolerably high scale, does not secure the markets of the protected country from invasion.[1] When her tariff duties were almost at the highest level, the United States were importing over a million tons of iron and steel annually, mainly from Great Britain, not occasionally, but for years together, and paying thereon duties to the extent of from half a million to a million and a half sterling annually. Even within the last few years the same country has imported an average of close on a million tons a year for two consecutive years. In the former case the iron imported was largely able to compete with that produced in home establishments, because the cost of production was so high. In the latter case the Americans could have produced iron and steel as cheaply as it was then or since produced in any foreign country, but the demand was so great that it had to be met from some source, and prices were so high that the imported iron had but little difficulty in securing access.[2] German experience, *mutatis mutandis*, has confirmed that of the United States. In the years 1899 and 1900, American iron and steel manufacturers invaded German markets to an extent that would not have been believed possible only a year or two before, and the danger of this invasion becoming persistent

[1] Statement prepared on behalf of the British Iron Trade Association for the Tariff Commission of 1903.
[2] For the two years ended October, 1903, the American prices of pig iron were 30s. to 40s. per ton higher than the average of Great Britain.

and more or less permanent, led to serious apprehensions on the part of the iron trade of the Fatherland, and to a considerable agitation with a view to the invaders being repelled. Indeed, there were at one time proposals under discussion on the part of the protected countries of continental Europe to take concerted action in order to shut out American iron and steel products.

The history of the iron trade has also made it perfectly clear that protected countries do not necessarily maintain a higher average range of prices than they would be likely to do under free trade. During the last half-century there has been no event in the history of prices that was so abnormal and so sensational as the rise that took place in this country towards the end of 1871, and continued until about the end of 1873. During that period the average price of pig iron rose about 150 per cent., and the prices of finished iron and steel rose to a corresponding extent. On the other hand, in the United States, at a time when a high-tariff policy was in vogue, the prices of both iron and steel fell to a lower level than anything known in the free-trade experience of Great Britain, except under more or less panic conditions.[1] In the former case free trade did not prevent British prices from reaching and maintaining an abnormally high range for a considerable period, and in the latter case, avowed and general protection did not hinder domestic products from falling to a level that has been almost without precedent in the history of price movements. It has been much the same in other high-tariff countries. Few of them have escaped occasional periods of depression when iron and steel products have been sold, despite high tariff duties, at prices that could hardly have been lower under any possible system of free trade.

[1] Bessemer or hematite pig iron sold for less than 40s. at Pittsburg, and Southern pig iron for less than 30s. per ton, in the period 1896-7.

It has been argued that the effect of protection is to maintain a greater uniformity of prices than would be possible under free trade, because home markets, not being so liable to sudden breaks by invading movements on the part of outside countries, are less likely to become demoralised and subject to unnatural fluctuations. The history of important protected markets like Germany and the United States hardly supports this view of the matter. On the contrary, the range of prices within those markets has fluctuated enormously.

Take the case of the United States as typically illustrative. Within the last thirty years the selling price of American pig iron has been as high as £12, and as low as 30s. per ton. The profits placed to the credit of the American ironmaker have been as much as 160s. per ton, and as low as 2s. 8d. These figures are given on the authority of the Eastern (U.S.) Ironmasters' Association, and are official, however improbable they may appear. The same extraordinary fluctuations have taken place in the values of raw material. In the period 1850–76, the cost of coal per ton of iron has been as high as 30s. and as low as 13s.; the cost of ore has been as high as 60s. and as low as 22s.; and the cost of labour has been as high as 22s. and as low as 7s. These variations of cost suggest the possibility that similar differences of range may occur in the future, and that history will more or less repeat itself.

The wide range of difference in cost of production as well as in selling prices, is strikingly illustrated in two tables found in the *Proceedings of the Institution of Civil Engineers* for 1899. These tables take the form of estimates of American and British hematite pig iron costs in that year, as presented by Messrs. Jeremiah and A. P. Head :—

COST OF PIG IRON PER TON AT PITTSBURG

	£	s.	d.
1·66 tons of ore at 12s. 8d.	1	1	1
16 cwt. of coke at 7s.	0	5	7
12 cwt. of limestone at 3s.	0	1	9½
Labour	0	2	0
Repairs	0	1	0
Other items .	0	1	0
	£1	12	5½

The following was the computed cost of producing pig iron on the Tees at the same time :—

COST OF PIG IRON PER TON AT MIDDLESBROUGH-ON-TEES

	£	s.	d.
1·95 tons of ore at 15s. 2d.	1	9	7
20·5 cwt. of coke at 15s. 6d.	0	15	10½
9 cwt. of limestone at 3s. 9d.	0	1	8½
Labour	0	3	0
Repairs	0	1	0
Other items .	0	1	0
	£2	12	2

The average price of pig iron in the United States in 1902, according to figures presented in the *Iron Age*, has been from $21 to $23 per ton, or, say, $22 over all. This corresponds to 89s. 10d. per ton, or nearly 60s. in excess of the cost of production at Pittsburg, as ascertained by the Messrs. Head in 1899. In other words, the total realised value of the 17,821,307 tons of pig iron produced in the United States in 1902 would be about £56,000,000 sterling in excess of the computed average cost of 1899, as typified by the Pittsburg figures above quoted !

I have elsewhere stated[1] that in most protectionist countries arrangements are in force whereby the prices of iron and steel are regulated by syndicates, or so-called

[1] Lectures delivered before the Faculty of Commerce, Birmingham University, 1902.

"cartels," and they may be fixed at any level that the producer may determine, within the limits permitted by the tariff. Practically, in the United States it is the action of the Steel Corporation that governs the prices of iron ore, coke, pig iron, and finished products. In Germany prices are similarly governed by syndicates in every important branch of the iron industry. In Austria-Hungary the cartel system of uniform regulated prices has recently been applied to practically every iron-manufacturing concern in the country. The same system is in operation in France and other ironmaking countries. In effect, therefore, it may be said that the prices of iron and steel are subject to the control of the producers in every country except our own. Here they are subject to such control only as foreign competition will permit.

While, therefore, foreign countries can always, subject to the limitations imposed by their respective tariffs, raise or lower prices at will to their home consumers, this country has no such liberty, but must largely be content with the prices determined by the surpluses which competitive countries like Germany and the United States dump on our shores, in order to keep their industries fully occupied. This principle has been carried so far that some two or three years ago it was admitted in Germany that in one important case the loss made by selling surplus abroad—mainly in British markets—was almost as large as the profit realised by sales in the German home markets. Quite recently an organisation by German manufacturers entered into a compact to reimburse the losses of those of their number who shipped iron and steel to this country at less than the cost of production.

It would not be proper to leave this important question here. Two things have to be admitted as fundamental in the history of customs tariffs as affecting the iron trade —the first, that they aid in the building up of home industries—under artificial conditions, no doubt, but still effectively ; and the second, that they give confidence and encouragement to capital. As a notable example of the former influence, it is only necessary to refer to the history since 1890 of the American tin-plate industry, which, almost without existence previous to that year, has in the interval attained proportions now fully equal to those of the Mother Country. The whole career of the American and German iron industries supplies most convincing and unequivocal proofs of the second influence named.

But the matter can be put in a form that seems to admit of no successful confutation. The country which, like our own, admits the products of all other countries free of duty, has no reliable control over its own home markets. The imports of iron and steel into Great Britain in each of the last two years averaged about 22 per cent. of our total home consumption, which is rather under 6,000,000 tons a year. Hence it may be argued that the foreign nations that send us this large quantity of iron and steel, supply their own home markets, within narrow limits at any rate, and about one-fifth, more or less, of the British markets as well. It is perfectly true that no nation absolutely supplies its own home market, since all alike import greater or less quantities of even the most heavily taxed commodities ; but the argument is sufficiently enforced by the fact that while Great Britain now imports an average of more than a million tons a year, no other producing nation imports one-half of that quantity, taking one year with another.

CHAPTER XXI

THE COMMERCIAL OUTLOOK OF THE
IRON TRADE

THE iron trade does not often attract within its pale men who have not been trained in its commerce and technique. There is good reason for this condition of things. Very few businesses are so entirely dependent upon both technical and commercial knowledge, and few require a greater amount of experience in order to be successful.

In this respect conditions are very different from what they were half a century ago, or even at a considerably later date. Then everything was more or less done by rule of thumb. "Whatever is, is right," was a common standard to work by. The pig-iron-maker worked by the eye alone. Fracture and not composition was his standard. The steel-manufacturer followed a system equally empirical. His idea of excellence was "body," and no one has yet succeeded in presenting a really intelligent or scientific description of this mysterious quality, which, nevertheless, entirely governed the operations and the aspirations of the crucible-steel producer of less than half a century ago.

To-day all this is changed. Science has not only invaded the field, but has practically controlled and held it. Chemical analysis is the universal solvent and determinant of character, quality, and value. Mechanical tests supply complementary information. Both are carried out under exact and severe technical conditions, from which there is usually no appeal.

The new *régime* requires that the successful ironmaker and steel-manufacturer shall be a capable chemist, metallurgist, geologist, physiographist, engineer, and a good many more things besides. No business or profession in existence calls for a higher standard of general scientific attainment.

From a commercial point of view the qualities demanded are almost equally exacting. As he is likely to have to do business with foreign countries, the up-to-date and fully equipped ironmaster is expected to have a knowledge of foreign languages, to be familiar with the currency, the special wants, the systems of exchanges, etc., and the tariffs of those countries. He must be keenly alive to the competitive circumstances of other countries. He must be something of a diplomatist and tactician, in order that he may successfully handle large bodies of workmen. He must be skilled in accountancy, seeing that his costs from day to day and from week to week have to be worked out to minute decimal points. He must be self-reliant and capable of dealing with such emergencies as the gobbing of a blast furnace, the breakage of rolls, or an accident at the boilers, the engines, the mills, or elsewhere. He must have such knowledge of affairs as will enable him to reach a sound judgment on the question of how far he would gain or lose by the many arrangements and combinations in which he is invited to join his fellow-manufacturers and in other suggestions that involve either individual or united action on critical occasions. He must also have the command of considerable means.

These few reflections make it clear that the iron trade is not to be taken up as a refuge for the destitute and the incapable. Let us now see what are the promises of reward held out to those who meet the necessary conditions of fitness and experience.

It may in general terms be laid down as an irrefragable principle that a business which presents chances of making considerable losses by the incompetent also opens up the prospect of large gains to the capable and deserving. Such, at least, is a correct description of the outlook of the iron trade. There is, however, one qualification necessary to this general statement. The iron trade is full of surprises, and as the wisest cannot always avoid disappointments, so the most foolish cannot always be submerged. Periods of good trade and bad trade bring results that are more or less beyond human control, and if in the fat years profits almost inevitably come to all, so in lean years only the discreet and the prudent will be able to minimise losses by having adequate reserves.

Among the many notable changes of the British iron trade during recent years the decreased supply of home ores, the decreased output of puddled iron, and the increased output of open-hearth steel, are the most striking. The Cleveland district is more or less a microcosm of the whole country in reflecting these movements. The greatest output of ore in this region was 6,750,000 tons, reached in 1883. Since then the output has fallen to an average of less than 5,500,000 tons a year. The make of puddled iron within much the same interval has fallen from over 850,000 tons to less than 200,000 tons a year ; and the output of open-hearth steel has increased from 6,000 tons to over 1,000,000 tons a year. But perhaps the most notable thing of all is the decline of the output of Bessemer steel from 485,000 tons in 1887 to less than 330,000 tons a year, averaging the last three years.

The fluctuations that are liable to take place in exports are indicated by the following figures, which set out the annual quantities shipped from British ports to foreign countries within the last five years :—

MAXIMUM AND MINIMUM EXPORTS TO LEADING
EUROPEAN COUNTRIES

			Maximum. Tons.		Minimum. Tons.
Russia, North	.	.	164,245	...	46,877
Russia, South	.	.	76,003	...	45,774
Germany	.	.	559,372	...	256,193
Holland	.	.	417,711	...	162,611
Belgium	.	.	165,145	...	75,208
France	.	.	181,093	...	92,177
Sweden	.	.	140,583	...	103,828
Norway	.	.	70,568	...	53,316
Denmark	.	.	76,926	...	49,649
Italy	.	.	185,715	...	139,531
Spain	.	.	34,207	...	15,564

Here, it will be seen, there has in most cases been a variation within this period of more than 100 per cent. Under such conditions business becomes extremely difficult, and this difficulty is almost always present to the iron- and steel-manufacturer. But it can, at least, be added that if his hopes are often disappointed it sometimes happens that his most sanguine expectations are realised.

The vicissitudes to which all iron- and steel-manufacturing businesses are liable are not limited to any one country or to any particular system of tariff policy. Great Britain, on the whole, shows less fluctuation than either the United States or Germany, but he would be a bold man who should assert that this fact is necessarily a function of her tariff system.

In a recent interesting article to the American Press, Mr. Carnegie made the following pertinent, if not entirely accurate statement :—

"At present the mines of ironstone and of coking coal in Britain are worked to their fullest capacity, and yet the output is not greatly increased; it is the same with those of Germany, except that in the latter country there remain some inferior fields capable of development if prices rise, as is probable. Russia, so far, has not been much of a factor in steel-making; if she is able to supply her own wants by the middle of the century she will be doing well. Except by the United States, Britain, and Germany, little steel is made, nor is any other nation likely to make much. The hopes in regard to China and Japan making steel, the writer believes, are to prove delusive. Britain and Germany cannot manufacture much beyond what they do now, so that the increased wants of the world can be met only by the United States. The known supply of suitable ironstone here is sufficient to meet all possible demands of the world for at least half of the century; in the case of coke for the entire century. It is not to be supposed that other deposits will not be discovered before known supplies are exhausted."

The outlook is likely to be materially affected by the extent to which new sources of raw material may shortly be discovered in the leading countries, by the movement of wages, by the efficiency and mobility of labour, by the incidence of standing charges, and by other minor considerations the conjoint and cumulative influence cf which must be considerable, although individually they do not perhaps count for much.

In Great Britain the average profits are not so considerable as they are in some other countries, and it is probable that they will relatively diminish, for two reasons—the first, because the expenditure on repairs, renewals, and reconstruction is not sufficient to keep plants up to the highest point of efficiency; and the second, because a sufficient amount of the gross profits has not generally been allocated to the risks of manufacturing accidents, renewals, and sales. In the United States, the capital expenditure is so large, owing to frequent replacement and reconstruction, that interest charges alone are put at 8s. to

8s. 6d. per ton, while for the risks that have just been named the highest authorities declare that another equal amount should be set aside. Here, then, we have a total of 16s. to 17s. per ton, provided in the United States to meet these necessary charges as a matter of common business prudence. It is probable that in Great Britain the amount so set aside is not half as much. Nor is it easy to increase it in view of the narrow margin of profit on which British manufacturers have usually to work.

In considering the outlook for Great Britain, one cannot overlook the fact that while countries like the United States, with a home market of large extent, practically secured to them by a high-tariff wall, have opportunities for the disposal of their surpluses all over the world, this country has neither home nor foreign markets that can be absolutely relied on except within very narrow limits. Hence the American, and to a large extent the German, manufacturer can depend on marketing his product within much wider limits of demand than his British compeer. I have elsewhere[1] stated that some friends of my own have only one reply to make to those who suggest lack of enterprise and apparent contentment with small yields—there is no market to rely on that would justify our producers of iron and steel in following American lines. This is no doubt true, with reservations. There is no obvious reason why, if we are to make iron at all, we should not make it under the best and most economical conditions possible to us. We could hardly lose anything if we raised the productiveness of our plants, reduced the number of hands employed for a given output of iron or steel, and got a larger annual production per unit of capital invested.

Much of the history of the future must depend on the

[1] Lecture delivered in connection with the Faculty of Commerce, Birmingham University.

extent to which the consumption of iron and steel is increased. It is difficult to make a confident forecast on this matter, all the more so that in various communities the annual consumption *per capita* of iron and steel ranges from only 4 lb. per head to over 500 lb. It is, however, to be presumed, as iron is, next to food, the greatest necessity of civilised life, that the consumption must largely and steadily increase in countries with a minimum consumption. My friend Mr. Edward Atkinson has prophesied that by 1910 the annual consumption of iron throughout the world will be fully fifteen million tons more than it was in 1900, and I am disposed to think he does not exaggerate. If so, and if the rate of increase continues, it may easily be that in the not far distant future there will be an iron famine, calling for the supply of greatly inferior ores to those now used.

APPENDIX

EXPORTS OF PIG IRON AND OF FINISHED IRON AND STEEL BY THE THREE CHIEF PRODUCING COUNTRIES, 1897 TO 1903, IN THOUSANDS OF TONS

GREAT BRITAIN

Year.	Pig Iron.	Semi-products.	Rails and Sleepers.	Merchant Iron and Steel and Girders.	Wire.	Plates.	Galvanised Plates.	Black Plates.	Tin-Plates.	Old Iron.	Totals.
1897 . .	1,220	Not separately stated.	795	474	52	121	231	60	276	89	3,318
1898 . .	1,059		620	444	45	103	230	59	256	87	2,902
1899 . .	1,401		601	496	50	112	242	87	261	118	3,368
1900 . .	1,451		471	473	39	86	251	67	278	97	3,213
1901 . .	853		633	337	48	77	254	52	276	87	2,617
1902 . .	1,121		729	433	56	85	337	58	317	104	3,241
1st half 1903	605	11	413	132	30	107	180	32	151	82	1,743
2nd ,, ,,	460	2	315	154	30	98	172	33	142	60	1,466

GERMANY

Year.	Pig Iron.	Semi-products.	Rails and Sleepers.	Merchant Iron and Steel and Girders.	Wire.	Plates.	Galvanised Plates.	Black Plates.	Tin-Plates.	Old Iron.	Totals.
1897 . .	91	40	147	414	201	—	138	—	—	38	1,069
1898 . .	187	35	155	468	191	—	158	—	—	85	1,279
1899 . .	182	23	140	415	157	—	158	—	—	53	1,129
1900 . .	129	34	195	388	173	—	175	—	—	61	1,155
1901 . .	150	202	224	672	252	—	264	—	—	153	1,917
1902 . .	347	636	416	743	237	—	284	—	—	169	2,832
1st half 1903	251	347	263	400	127	—	152	—	—	61	1,570
2nd ,, ,,	170	301	187	365	127	—	139	—	—	49	1,370

UNITED STATES

Year.	Pig Iron.	Semi-products.	Rails and Sleepers.	Merchant Iron and Steel and Girders.	Wire.	Plates.	Galvanised Plates.	Black Plates.	Tin-Plates.	Old Iron.	Totals.
1897 . .	267	6	150	15	54	—	9	—	—	60	561
1898 . .	257	29	306	35	76	—	32	—	—	62	797
1899 . .	232	26	272	112	118	—	57	—	—	77	894
1900 . .	291	109	367	173	79	—	55	—	—	49	1,123
1901 . .	81	29	318	107	88	—	31	—	—	14	668
1902 . .	27	2	67	110	98	—	18	—	2	9	332
1st half 1903	8	0	4	50	53	—	10	—	—	2	137
2nd ,, ,,	9	1	24	33	57	—	11	—	—	4	135

INDEX

Q   225